National Theatre Connections Monologues

Anthony Banks is a theatre director who was born in Manchester, studied directing at the Royal Academy of Dramatic Art in London and has worked all over the UK. He was an associate director at the National Theatre of Great Britain for ten years where he commissioned and developed a hundred NT Connections plays.

Connections is the National Theatre's festival of new plays for youth theatres and schools. It began in 1995 when teachers and directors told the NT that they wanted exciting and challenging new plays for young actors to perform. Since then the NT has commissioned and published more than 160 plays for Connections, giving young people aged 13–19 across the UK and Ireland access to the very best of new writing for theatre.

Whether you're a school, youth theatre or voluntary organisation, whether you're experienced theatre-makers or have never staged a production before, your group can apply to be part of Connections. You'll have support from the National Theatre and the chance to perform your production at a Connections Festival in leading theatres across the UK.

To find out more please go to connections.nationaltheatre.org.uk

National Theatre Connections Monologues

Speeches for Young Actors

Edited by

ANTHONY BANKS

methuen | drama

LONDON · NEW YORK · OXFORD · NEW DELHI · SYDNEY

METHUEN DRAMA
Bloomsbury Publishing Plc
50 Bedford Square, London, WC1B 3DP, UK

BLOOMSBURY, METHUEN DRAMA and the Methuen Drama logo
are trademarks of Bloomsbury Publishing Plc

First published in Great Britain 2016
Reprinted 2016, 2017, 2018 (twice)

A catalogue record for this book is available from the British Library

ISBN: PB: 978-1-4725-7310-0
ePDF: 978-1-4725-7312-4
ePub: 978-1-4725-7313-1

A catalog record for this book is available from the Library of Congress

Typeset by RefineCatch Limited, Bungay, Suffolk
Printed and bound in Great Britain

To find out more about our authors and books visit www.bloomsbury.com
and sign up for our newsletters.

With thanks to . . .

After Juliet by Sharman Macdonald (reproduced by permission of Faber and Faber Ltd)

Blooded by Isabel Wright (reproduced with permission of Capercaillie Books)

Burying Your Brother in the Pavement by Jack Thorne (reproduced with permission of Nick Hern Books)

DNA by Dennis Kelly (reproduced with permission of Oberon Books)

Friendly Fire by Peter Gill (reproduced with permission of Faber and Faber)

Gizmo by Alan Ayckbourn (reproduced with permission of Faber and Faber)

Little Foot by Craig Higginson (reproduced by permission of Oberon Books Ltd)

Pronoun by Evan Placey (reproduced with permission of Nick Hern Books)

Same by Deborah Bruce (reproduced with permission of Nick Hern Books)

Too Fast by Douglas Maxwell (reproduced with permission of Oberon Books)

The Wardrobe by Sam Holcroft (reproduced with permission of Nick Hern Books)

Contents

Introduction

When you're starting out as an actor, you'll find yourself in a situation where you have to present your talent and skills on your own, in a room or on a stage. Acting, like everything else in the theatre profession, is an inherently *collaborative* activity – you collaborate with the other actors, your director, the words you are given to speak, the design of the production, and of course with the audience – but as well as being a fantastic collaborator, you'll also be required to demonstrate how you *personally* respond and interpret text which has been written for performance, and the hundred speeches in this book are here to enable you to do that.

I imagine if you're reading this book, you'll either be preparing a speech for an audition of some sort, or you'll be working on a monologue in order to explore the many different ways you can bring it to life, as a way of learning how to be a good actor. Actors have been working in this way for thousands of years: when western drama began in Ancient Greece, the actors had to prepare long speeches and perform them in front of thousands of people in huge open air amphitheatres. In those days, the play and the performance relied almost entirely on actors speaking words that had been written by dramatists. The audience's attention and imagination was captured by the words the actor spoke, the way they expressed them and the stories they told. The discipline of getting your head and heart around a speech that has been written to be performed can be one of the most thrilling, terrifying, releasing and immensely satisfying challenges any artist can have.

In order to help you harness your nerves and ignite your imagination, I asked half a dozen leading actors to give their tips for preparing speeches, this is what they said:

Benedict Cumberbatch:
"Read it again and again. Mine the material for all its worth. Sit with it and ask all the page 1 acting questions of your character and the situation and the writer. Only then start learning it. Then you are learning the why as well as the how. Try to work it through with another person for objective distance and the ability to not get in your own way with the material. There's nothing better for not over thinking a piece than having an audience and an outside eye. Go through it with ANYONE patient enough to do that with you! You need to lose your inhibitions as you can only learn by failing and it's better to do that outside of the audition. Loneliness and failure often fire the imagination. But there's nothing like having an outside eye to help you realize your full potential. Go into the audition

remembering they want you to succeed and get the job. They are already on your side. If you give them what they aren't expecting they should, if they have any generosity of spirit, give you the opportunity to change direction. If you can hear what they say and act on their words through the adrenaline rush of having performed in front of them and all your internal voices of doubt and fear then be sure, even if you are not right for them this time, your work with them will be remembered. Good luck!"

Helen George:
"It sounds obvious, but after you've chosen your speech, don't be lazy: read the play!
    Don't try and wing it, you'll always get found out . . ."

Cush Jumbo:
"Learn it. Learn it again. Learn it upside down and back to front. Learn it until the words become your own and not someone else's oh and . . . LEARN IT!"

Rory Kinnear:
"Learn your lines. Learn them so well you don't have to think about them. Learn them so that they're in your body and not in your brain. So you're thinking of everything those lines mean and not what they are. That means going over them again and again. It's boring. But once they're in – you are free to do with them whatever you want. And that is exhilarating."

Andrea Riseborough:
"Choose a something you love. If you can't choose, find something to love about what you've been given."

Jemima Rooper:
"Do it everywhere. You can't do it enough. Don't care who sees you. You may get sectioned but you will be so used to doing it that when you're under pressure it will come from your bones. I'm talking about a speech, I promise."

    I resisted putting the speeches into categories because most of them can be spoken by girls or boys, and by most ages in the 13–19 range. I chose a variety of different lengths of speeches, something for each and every challenge and occasion. I encourage you to read the speeches and seek out the plays I have taken them from in order to find a speech which really fires you.

                                                                    Anthony Banks

The Accordion Shop

Cush Jumbo

Mister Ellody, his father and his grandfather before him, have kept their family business going for generations on the high street. When a riot breaks out and teenagers start looting the shops on the street, they steal trainers, iPods, anything they can get their hands on. The one shop that remains untouched is Mister Ellody's and the precious accordions inside. This is an ensemble play in which a large group of young actors play all the characters who are involved in the incident on the street.

Mister Ellody   Do you have any idea what an accordion is worth? I sell the most expensive items on the whole of The Road. Beautiful, hand-made, antique, one of a kind instruments and they weren't even looking twice, they didn't care. I saw one boy running away with a mis-matched pair of Adidas trainers. Idiot I thought. You bloody idiot. One of these accordions would buy you five hundred pairs of those.

It's not the money, I make enough of that. I repair accordions from all over the world, I have a waiting list of two years. But sometimes . . . when my Dad was alive the shop was full of life. People would come in just to see and touch and hear the music, otherwise what's the point? The only person that seems to show any interest now is the lady across the road, she brings me a cup of tea everyday and I don't even know her name. I'd never leave The Road but sometimes when those kids chuck their chicken boxes in my doorway, or graffiti on my window, or pass by without even noticing the beautiful instruments inside, yes I do feel like leaving. I feel like giving up. I get angry and this hot scratchy air fills up my throat until I can't breathe and it's trapped in there and I don't know what to do.

Children used to be so excited by the mystery of things, I know I was. Watching my Dad build an accordion was like watching a wizard cast a spell. He'd make the bellows by intricately pleating layer after layer of cloth and cardboard, cloth and cardboard. I'd never take my eyes off his hands as he closed up the wooden body for the last time because I knew I'd probably never see the inside of that accordion again. What I'd seen was a one off. It made me feel special. I'd wanted to pass that on to someone else but unfortunately I don't have any children.

You have many choices in the way you create this character. How old is he? Where is he from? Does he have a European accent? Italian perhaps? Is he talking directly to the audience? Who does he think they are? Why does he think they want to listen to him? The character could, of course, also be played as a woman shopkeeper.

After Juliet

Sharman Macdonald

Shortly after the deaths of Romeo and Juliet, there is an uneasy truce between the Montague and Capulet families, and Benvolio, Romeo's friend, has fallen in love with Rosaline. Here Rosaline visits Juliet's grave with some flowers, in the corner of a piazza.

Rosaline   Your spirit haunts me Juliet.
I see more of you dead
Than I did when you were alive;
That's a joke. 'More of you dead.' Go on laugh.
And more of you alive than I wanted to.
Laugh. Laugh, go on.
Come on Juliet.
We were hardly close as cousins.
You were too small, too pretty, too rich,
Too thin and too much loved for me to cope with.
'Spoilt' is the word that springs to mind
Though I don't want to speak ill of the dead.

She touches one of the flowers she is holding.

All a flower does is wither
It's the memories that stay forever:
So they tell me.
So what do I recall of you?
Juliet, daddy's princess, rich
Mummy's darling, quite a bitch.
You scratched my face once
From here to here
I have the scar. I have it yet
You can see it quite clearly.
In the sunlight;
A silver line.
You wanted my favourite doll.
And of course you got it
For though I was scared, you cried.
And your nurse swooped down
And took the moppet from me.

Spanked me hard for making you unhappy
Gave my doll to you, her dearest baby.
Later you stole my best friend
Wooed her with whispers;
Told her gossip's secrets;
Gave her trinkets, sweetmeats.
Later still, you took my love
And didn't know you'd done it;
Then having taken him
You let him die.

If you'd swallowed the friar's potion earlier
You would have wakened.
And my love would be alive.
None of this would have happened.
I know you, Juliet
You hesitated, frightened.
Didn't take the stuff until the dawn.
Wakened too late in the tomb.
In the night I dream of Romeo.
He's reaching his arms out from the vault.
The poison has him in its hold.
He fills my nights with his longing for life
Until I am afraid to go to sleep
For though I love him still
I cannot soothe his pain.
If I could, I would
But it is not me he's reaching for.
So why Juliet
Should I spend my cash
On flowers for you?
Are you a saint
Simply because you were daft enough
To die for love. Love?
A passing fancy, no more nor less.
Tomorrow or tomorrow or tomorrow
You would have tired of him.
Like your fancy for the doll.
Once possessed, you left it in the rain.
Yesterday's fancy, mud in its hair
Damp stained the dress I'd made for her.
They think you brave to have taken your life

But you believed in immortality.
Daddy's princess could not die.
She would be there at her own funeral
To watch the tears flow
And hear her praises sung.
So you haunt me.
Don't turn away.
Listen. Listen.
What is it that you've brought about?
What trail does your fancy drag behind?
What punishments lie in your fancy's wake?
Listen Juliet.
Come here. Come close
Press your ear to the earth
So I know you're listening.
There's a trial going on.
Even now. In all solemnity.
Four lives hang in the balance
Forced by your selfish suicide
To take their chance
Standing at the mercy of the court.
They wait to see whether life or death
Is granted them by what we call justice.
It's a strange justice. Law meted out by the rich
Who measure their wisdom
By the weight of their gold;
As if riches bear witness to virtue.
You and I know they don't.
So four poor people are brought before the Prince.
To see whether they live or die.
You brought this on them.
No feud wrought their trials
Their misery is tribute
To your precocity.
Married. And at thirteen!
So. So. Sweet Coz.
Here. This is the last flower
You'll get from me.
Death flowers have the sweetest scent.

She casts the flower down. Shrugs.

That's that bit done.

She puts down the umbrella. Stands with her face up to the rain.

You'll need to do quite a bit of preparation for this but it'll be worth it. As well as reading the sequel, you should also read the original Shakespeare play, Romeo and Juliet, and make sure that you can answer any questions that Rosaline might be asked, for example, who are the four people she talks about who are on trial? You are Juliet's cousin: she was married when she was thirteen years old, how old are you now? The speech is written in verse, note where the lines end and begin, this will help you to measure your way through and decide how each section should be interpreted.

Alice by Heart

Steven Sater and Duncan Sheik

This is an American rock musical about a young woman called Alice who is sheltering from the Blitz in London in the 1940s and who imagines that the Tube station where she is sleeping is the rabbit hole in which Lewis Carroll's Alice's Adventures in Wonderland takes place. In this scene, she is reunited with the crazed Duchess, who is even more unpleasant than when Alice first met her.

Duchess　　(*warm, maternal*) Now, you. Now, Piggie, come to Duchess.
　　All grown up, are you?
　　Not what I hear from youm –
　　wallowing through the afternoon,
　　trailing bunny tails and doing Shroooooooms?!

(*vicious*)

　　I can see it in your eyes, Pig.
　　I can smell it in your hair.
　　Now, now. You must look to your snout:
　　the more that comes out, the more to talk about.
　　The more that goes in, the porkier the chin.
　　But ohhhh, Piggie got so big!
　　Ohhhhh, she had to puff and grin to keep that pigtail in!
　　So, now you're all too big to be my pig!
　　Pig! You made yourself too big.
　　Grew yourself such breasts and hips,
　　my lovelies sagged, just watching them.
　　You ripped the plumpy from my rump
　　and left me this fat belching gut.
　　You broke my heart, you selfish tart,
　　and now my day's just fart fart fart!
　　And now my cheeks just leak! Leak! Leak!
　　You made my bed a dripping sink!
　　And so I'm left – with no one left.
　　You stole my soul and made me old, you pig!
　　You stripped the sheets and robbed my sleep
　　and left my youth a dream!

I'll see you at the trial!
You PIIIIIIIIIIIIIIG!!!!
PIIIIIIIIIIGGGGGGG!!!!!

You're a grotesque caricature of a woman who is seething with jealousy at the sight of the now adolescent Alice, who has the body of a young woman, rather than the body of the girl you saw the first time she fell down the rabbit hole. Have a look at the illustrations of The Duchess in Lewis Carroll's Alice's Adventures in Wonderland, which you'll be able to find online, for inspiration for this outrageous, sinister monster of a character.

Almost Grown

Richard Cameron

This play takes place in Yorkshire and is about blame, guilt and loss of innocence. At the centre of the story are three young men, all harbouring something that is slowly destroying them. The play has flashbacks that show them as younger men, and the flashback scenes inform the audience's understanding of the present. In the case of Tommy, he is grieving the loss of his mother, and he holds his abusive stepfather responsible for her death.

Tommy   I went to find him. Tell him what I thought of him. I was going to sort him. I thought I'd find somebody I wanted to sort for good. If he'd have laughed at me, smirked, tried to hit me again . . . it would have been easy. I could have done it easy, but he didn't do any of that. Didn't even turn away in shame or whatever. Just took it. Looking at me. Dead eyes. He was already dead, you know? Nothing. Nothing going on. Eddie was right. He was already . . . somebody else had done it for me. Mam had already done it for me, got in his head, started killing him slow, from the inside out. She didn't need me to do it for her.

They must have had something going on for 'em, between 'em, eh? You can't look like he looked and not have once felt something for somebody.

I couldn't even do him for me. For what he did to me. For years I've wanted to kill him and then when I'm there, the chance to do it, I don't want to any more. Like, I've grown up to meet him grown up and settle it, and I can't because he's got past being grown up, growing back down again to old. Little again. A little old man before his time. Bent. Like killing a baby. It's all in there, what he's done, but it's all turned to mush. His brain is already mush without me making it mush. I wanted to but she'd already done it for me.

To a great extent, you're thinking aloud; you're deducing in the moment. As you describe the extraordinary atmosphere that exists between you and your stepfather on the day you went to confront him, the memory of the power of that moment fuels your words. You must 'keep the lid on' –

that is, contain the raw energy of the memory inside the precision required to articulate precisely what you have to say in the present moment – if you get the balance of this, find the right level of internal tension, the speech will be convincing.

Angels

Pauline McLynn

A curious group of youngsters find themselves in protective overalls and masks, carrying out community service, cleaning-up a graveyard. Some of them are there because they have committed minor crimes, some are there voluntarily. As they clear up the rubbish and talk about what bothers them in their lives, three carved stone angels come to life and sing and watch over them. A boy called Shawn has been living in a tomb in the graveyard because his flat burned down, killing his mother and brother. Here he tells his story to the group assembled in the graveyard.

Shawn There was just my Mum and my kid brother. But, yeah, they both died.

Of lots of things. Poverty for one. And me, I let them down. Me, most of all.

We lived in this shitty little council house. My Dad's been gone years, anyone else just came and went without staying long. Mum was so exhausted all the time from working all these different shifts to make ends meet. On . . . *that* . . . day . . . I went out to get some milk and Mum fell asleep while she was cooking the dinner . . . the chip pan went on fire . . . and Mum and my little brother, Patrick, died in the blaze. He was two years old.

But I should have been there. If I had been there I could have saved them. If I had been there, it never would have happened.

A litre of milk. They died from overwork and . . .

I wouldn't have had to go for the milk if I hadn't had cereal in the middle of the afternoon . . . all because I was too lazy to make myself a sandwich.

This speech is spoken towards the end of the play. It is the middle of the night and everyone has crept into the graveyard with torches. The atmosphere is very eerie. Until this point, you have been a mysterious presence in the graveyard; the other characters have been obsessed about their own concerns, which melt almost into insignificance when they hear what has recently happened to you.

By talking about the tragic events that have overwhelmed you, you find that you begin to make a connection with the people around you and they become your new friends. Notice how the writer juxtaposes the trivia of everyday life, like sandwiches and milk, with life-changing events like the loss of a mother.

Asleep Under the Dark Earth

Sian Evans

This play follows the lives of two girls from different backgrounds in early nineteeth-century Wales. Nia is a farm labourer's daughter and Bethan is a landowner's daughter. They find they're both attracted to the same man, a young preacher called Caleb.

Bethan   Dear Lord, forgive me this morning the sins of yesterday.

Arrogance. I was rude to one of the servants, Joshua. I lost my temper. I thought I'd told him to repair my shoes by Sunday and then I realized that I had not but I scolded him anyway. Felt even worse. Thought of going to Joshua later and apologizing but did not.

Ingratitude. Resentment. Saw Nia talking to Mari. First time she's visited the house in two years. Ignored her. It pained me. I was being obedient to father, which is my first duty, but I felt that I have sinned in some other way. Felt angry towards father. Saw Nia's face. Hurt. Dreamed last night that we met, that we left the house together, that we had . . . changed again . . . flown away . . .

Regret. Yesterday longed for mother. Wanted to pluck her from eternal bliss and bring her back to me. Didn't care about her pain and suffering as long as she was here with me.

And I have sinned against our guest Caleb. Though I – cannot say how or why. I have felt no peace since he's been here. He's kind and polite, but when he talks to me I cannot answer. It's as though my tongue fills my mouth. I am frightened that he will think a slight. Last night father noticed too and gave me one of his black looks.

Forgive me. Fill me with love and understanding . . .

In this scene, which opens the play, you are discovered praying alone in the private chapel of your house. It is 1830. Think about what you'd be wearing, perhaps do some research about girls who were landowners' daughters living in rural Wales at that time. The speech is weighed down with the heaviness of guilt; think about how you are going to offer up that weight in your confession to the god you are praying aloud to.

Baby Girl

Roy Williams

*Sam has discovered that she's going to be a grandma at the age of 26.
She lives on an estate in South-East London with her daughter Kelle who
is 13 and pregnant. This speech takes place early one evening and Sam
has decided she needs a night out and some distraction. She's talking to
herself, alone in her bedroom.*

Sam   Mum? Sorry, love, there's no mum here. Mum is having the night
off. All that is left is Sam. Sam with the legs! That's what yer dad used to
say. You don't mind if I wear your dress do yer? Course you don't, sis! It
was way too sexy for you anyhow. I thought I told you to take it back,
like you listen to a word I say. What am I, yer mum?! I'm glad you didn't
take it back. It looks right on me, don't you think? It gives out just the
right signal. I am a dam waiting to burst.

Poor sod, whoever he is, won't know what's hit him, cos I feel like
chicken tonight! You don't mind me talking like that? Course you don't,
after all we're sisters! I'm really loving this, it's liberating, it's funny, I
feel young again, bring it on!

Borrowing your lip gloss, alright? I'll take you out next time, I promise.
When you've dropped yer load. Then we'll find out who is the best at
checking men. Course we already know, ca', gal, I'd wipe the floor wid
you. I got plenty, I am stacked. Yer gran's babysitting, don't argue, done
deal. Don't give her any lip. Listen to me, I sound like yer mother. Not
when I walk through that door I won't. Sam is back! Lock up yer boys,
mums! I shall be back, whenever.

*In this speech we see and hear a kind of flashback to the days when Sam
was a teenager. We get glimpses of what it was like when she lived with
her family and we start to see a picture of the cycle of teenage pregnancy
that the play presents. As you perform the speech you should imagine the
ghosts of your family members in the room as you refer to them, so that
each line lands somewhere very specific. The phrase 'I feel like chicken
tonight' is a joke borrowed from a television advert and the last line is a
riff on the phrase 'Lock up your daughters', which was a popular
musical in the 1960s.*

Bassett

James Graham

*This is about a class that has been locked in an upstairs classroom by a
supply teacher who has gone AWOL. Meanwhile, outside in the village of
Wootton Bassett, a repatriation procession is taking place in which the
body of a soldier known to the class is being brought home. This speech
closes the play; the atmosphere has become extremely heated, as
arguments about identity, faith and loyalty have broken out amongst the
class. Spencer has been ordered to face the wall for the majority of the
play, and this is where he stands.*

Spencer   (*still facing the wall*) And erm . . . 'course in the Second
World War, I think . . . I think a lot of people forget that we were the first
ones to declare war. On Germany. Not America or anyone. Or France. Or
. . . which, you know, I think . . . well, that's quite brave. Isn't it? Really.
We didn't want a war, says here, we were still a bit buggered from the
last one. But we saw someone doing something wrong to people.
Invading countries that didn't belong to them and doing bad things to the
people that lived there. And we thought . . . 'no, that . . . that's not right'.
And so we did something about it. And Hitler made us an offer to stay
out of it, which would have meant a lot of our granddads and grandmas
wouldn't have died and we'd be really powerful, but we still said no.
And by the time they got to us, we were like completely alone. And
everyone thought we would lose. But we didn't. And then it looks like
America came along, and finished it up, and then we owed them a lot of
money because we'd been fighting for so long on our own. And that
meant we lost our empire and have been shrinking and struggling a bit
ever since, never quite the same, but we knew that might happen and yet
we still did it. Because we thought we had a responsibility. And I think
that . . . you know. That's something that we should be, like, proud of. A
bit more. And something that we forget, when all this other stuff is
happening. Even when we get things wrong, and make mistakes. That if
it wasn't for us. On this island. Then, like, the world and all that, it would
be really quite bad right now. Worse than it is. And so . . . you know . . .

. . . that's what I've learnt, anyway. That we're better than we think we are.

And that we can do better, most of the time. If only we remembered that.

So I think we'll be all right, actually . . . you know, in the . . . in the, like, long run.

I do. I actually do . . .

You're a bit socially inept, but you're quick of mind and sometimes speak before you think. The effect of your speech within the context of the play is somewhat expressionist due to the circumstances in which you're speaking. This speech, delivered to the rest of his class, sits in the aftermath of a lengthy and violent argument between everyone in the class, so your voice is one of careful, relative calm and measured contemplation. The delivery style therefore should be trepidatious and pragmatic, and slightly knowing of the world outside the classroom: the audience's world.

The Bear Table

Julian Garner

A small group of teenagers venture into a forest near Helsinki, share a magic mushroom and fall asleep. When they wake it seems that the city has disappeared, that Aleksi's hand is bleeding and they are being chased by a bear. Aleksi then starts to talk backwards and finds that the others can only communicate with him if they talk backwards too. They find themselves at the house of a man in a bear suit, who invites them to eat with him, if they too put on bear suits. This surreal play is set in different parts of a huge forest in Finland.

Harri Dad? Dad, is that you? I've fallen down an old well in the forest, I've broken some ribs I think, I was running from a bear, it's freezing, Dad, I can't get out, I've tried, I'm starving, Dad, please, Dad, come and get me, it's near the old camp, Bloodnut's old camp, you know, there's a shark like a rock, I mean a rock like a shark, can you hear me? Dad? Dad? Can you hear me, I'm stuck here, you are there, aren't you? Dad? Dad? Dad! Dad! Dad! Dad! Dad!

The phone rings.

Shut up! You're not really ringing, it's just a dream. Shut up! Shut up! Your battery's flat, you can't be ringing! I said, shut up! Shut up! SHUT UP!! SHUT UP! SHUT UP! SHUT UP!

He answers it.

Hello? Aleksi?! But? You're at the camp?! I'm in a well, I think it's a well, I fell down it. It's about two hundred metres from where the flats used to be, two, three hundred metres. There's a rock that looks like a shark, I never saw it before, near there. Like a shark, yes, bursting out of the ground, there's trees on its back, but it looks like a shark. Are you really there, is it really you, Aleksi? It's so good to hear your voice, you know, I? Hello? Hello, Aleksi?? You're breaking up. Hello? Your voice? Can you see it?! Really, you can see it?! Like a shark, yeah, it's there, near there, be careful, it's very deep! I'll shout, perhaps you'll hear me. ALEKSI, THIS WAY! THIS WAY! DOWN HERE! ALEKSI! ALEKSI! HERE I AM! OVER HERE, DOWN HERE, OVER HERE! CAN'T YOU FIND IT? IT'S HERE! HERE! ALEKSI! ALEKSI?! HELP! HELP!

Harri, who can be played as a boy or a girl, has fallen into a deep well or pit somewhere in the forest. This speech requires you to show a mixture of confusion, fear and panic; the interesting thing for the audience will be watching your face as you process each tiny part of the predicament. In the first part of the speech you are trying to make a phone call and in the second part you are receiving one, and it could be the phone call that saves your life. In the final few lines, which are written in capital letters, you are shouting to Aleksi who is above ground at the top of the well you are trapped in.

The style of this play is very surreal; the challenge is to decide which elements of the speech you play in such a way that you anchor them in a realistic context; you can't play the whole speech with a frantic energy as it could become boring or difficult to follow. Try to find a way of presenting the journey of your character that starts in a state of traumatized danger leading to a realization that hope and rescue might be a real possibility.

The Bedbug

Snoo Wilson

This play is based on a Russian futurist play by Vladimir Mayakovsky called The Bedbug, written in 1929. The first half of the play takes place immediately after the Bolshevik Revolution in Moscow; the second half takes place in an imagined future, decades later, when the central character, Ivan Varlet, is defrosted and wakes up in a clinical world.

Mayakovsky   'In my end is my beginning.' Who am I? A poet. Right.
My first poem was 'Mayakovsky, a Tragedy',
I am Vladimir Mayakovsky, come from the dead.
Like other visitors from the nether world, my time here is brief.
Relax, I explain everything. The only brains blown out tonight will be
    mine.
For those who have not read their programmes yet
This prologue is pronounced by the shade
Of the former author – who long ago shot himself.
Some say I Mayakovsky knew
My time was up: Stalin was always behind a bad review.
My advice to you, is enjoy tonight! It could be your last, and any
    artistic shock
Could be a trembling prelude to delight.

The Bedbug; work of genius, begins in a street market after that false
    dawn of
The assassination of the Czar, the Russian Revolution ushering in
A brief and comically deluded season of hope.
Audience! Do your best. If not moved, pretend. To be alive
Is not always to be sincere; Unless you are a genius.
You might say I foresaw
The revolution would turn to ashes, and burnt straw.
I left a note, to be found beside my brains. 'The loveboat has crashed'.
Hell's devils tell me it loses everything, in translation.
– But they would, wouldn't they? –
The poetic heart is subject to perturbation.
My love life was not in tip top condition, plus
I was subject to arrest by Comrade Stalin
And the condemned man calls in vain for pen and paper.

I had a flair for gesture that enabled me to pinch out
My own deathless flame; – and what can I tell you? –
Darkness! No more taper.
My pen, you will observe skewers many hearts;
I wield it like a stake, to drive through the hypocritical left ventricle
    of all later Stalinist, Socialist-Realist, fear-beshitted so-called 'art'!
A glowing Futurist electron storm returns
To illuminate the tundra of the Russian soul!
I hereby conjure up before your eyes
A Russian state department store
In front of it here, a People's Market.
(*Effects begin.*) Begin my play, and
Unfold here, its lethal prophecy.

*Everything that Mayakovsky does and says is larger than life. He is
opening a play, and what's more, it's his own play, which has been
re-invented to give a layer of meaning that wasn't available when he
wrote it as he had set his play in a future that has now passed. This is a
verbal firework display, and it requires a huge amount of planning and
then a huge amount of energy to perform it.*

The Black Remote

Glyn Maxwell

*This is a poetic fantasy based on the myth of Pandora and her box,
which contains the spirits of good and evil. It is set in a kingdom that
is slightly futuristic, and follows the adventures of three sisters whose
parents have gone off travelling. The parents leave a list of things
the girls must not do, which includes the instruction 'Do not use the
black remote'. Polly, one of the sisters, does use the black remote
and switches on a massive screen from which emerge three monsters
representing fame, snobbery and indifference, who turn the town into
a war zone. The style of this play is non-realist. You are the youngest
of three sisters and you're talking to a statue that has just come to
life. Sitting nearby is a strange, winged creature called Nono. This
speech comes at a pivotal point in the play when you realize the
enormity of your mistake with the remote and wonder how you and
your friend, Norman, will ever be able to rectify the situation you have
created.*

Polly   His dream is coming true . . .
But his dream was down to us. We let that creature
out, and Norman thinks it's the right creature,
not the wrong creature . . . I don't know what to think.
I'm talking to a Statue, so it's clear
I don't know what to think!
Vehicles are moving, they have guns
on top of them, swinging this way and that.
Crowds are following, men with flames and sticks . . .
Can that be the right creature?
But they're doing it all for beauty. I suppose
if they tell the people living in the houses
it's being done for beauty, that might work,
those people would understand and say alright,
it's being done for beauty, we'll move off.
We'll go and live in a place you want us to.
Then there won't be any fighting.
They only have to say it, the Army:

we're doing this for beauty,
and the people will collect their pots and pans,
their souvenirs and satchels,
and go while there's still time.
They only have to say it.
I think they didn't say it. I think they didn't
say it in any language.
Now everything is alive
and everything is fighting, and it's me,
I let it happen – Norman, the black remote –
when they said I was not to touch it,
I did and I let it happen. I let the wrong
creature out and he let the right one out
but now it's wrong and stone men came to life
and all in all I wish my mum and dad
would find themselves and bring themselves home
where I am, because, because – no one's found me.

Nono – what about him? Is he the answer?
But he just hangs there singing, he does nothing,
he doesn't mind, he's easy. How could he matter?
And how could the answer to anything be in an attic?
It's all the things that are over,
things sitting there forever,
things that are sad and dusty and pathetic,
poor Nono, stuck in there.
Now there's no one else the singing could be.
Nono? Your wings . . . They look too big to fly with.
Now it's quiet and he's listening but now
I've nothing to say to him.
Except I do keep thinking:
in every story I read when I read stories,
it was the third thing that mattered. The young one,
or the ugly one or the poor one got the treasure.
Things went in threes, and these three, they were things,
weren't they. Two have gone, and . . . Nono?
Do you want to hear the news?
We let them out, those others, and between them,
Nono, they ruined everything. It's our fault.
We used the black remote.
What do you think of that?

It is a speech about coming to terms with responsibility. Although it is a very descriptive speech you should perform it with the heavy weight of the consequences of your actions present in your voice.

Blackout

Davey Anderson

This is about a Glaswegian teenager, but it could be performed in any accent. The story is about how he falls in with the wrong crowd and ends up committing a terrible crime. The whole play is told by him in flashbacks in which he keeps returning to the moment he was first locked up in a police station cell.

James Imagine
　　You wake up
　　You open your eyes
　　And you're like that
　　Where am I?
　　A small room
　　Bright lights
　　White walls
　　A metal door
　　Oh my god!
　　Imagine you wake up and you're in a jail cell.
　　You go up to the door.
　　You bang your fists.
　　Screaming
　　Shouting
　　What am I doing in here?
　　And imagine the polis guy comes up to the door.
　　And he's like that
　　Keep it doon.
　　And you're like
　　Whit did I dae?
　　Aw, do you not know?
　　You shake your head.
　　Whit?
　　And the polis guy just looks at you like you're a pure thug or something.
　　Imagine he just looks at you and he goes
　　You're getting charged with attempted murder, wee man.
　　You'd be like that
　　Aw naw
　　What did I do?
　　And you'd start remembering

Everything
Right from the beginning
You would try to remember
How did I get here?

So you'd start remembering your dad.
He was a woman beater.
He beat up your mum every day
From the day they got married right up to the day they got divorced.
He used to beat her to a pulp.
So she stopped working.
She wouldn't go out the house.
Cos she was embarrassed.
She didn't want to walk down the street with her face all black and blue.
And you'd remember that your ma didnae want you to grow up to be
    like him.
She wanted you to be a famous lawyer
Or a famous doctor
Or a famous whatever.
And you'd remember that you were poor.
But you weren't poor poor.
Cos your mum still made sure there was a dinner on the table every
    night.
She'd give you her last penny
She didn't care about herself.
But you'd remember that you never really spoke to her.
Cos you'd come home from school and go straight up the stairs.
James?
Aye.
Your dinner's out.
You'd come down.
Grab the plate.
Thanks, ma.
Back up the stairs.
So you never really spoke to her.

But you'd remember your granddad.
He was the closest thing you had to a proper father.
He put you under his wing.
He did everything a dad would do.
He'd hold your hand
He'd walk you down to the shops
He'd play daft wee games with you

But best of all, he'd take you to the Rangers game every Saturday.
He'd take you to see the Orange Walks.
You'd remember how he taught you to play the flute.
But you'd not to play The Sash
Or hang the Ulster flag out the window.
He taught you to keep that kind of thing to yourself.
But then he got his cancer.
You'd remember that.
So every night you'd go and sit with him.
Play a game of cards
Help him do a jigsaw
Have a cup of tea and look out the back window.
You'd remember that that was where the boys fae your scheme used
    to fight with the boys fae the scheme doon the road.
They'd run at each other with bottles and bricks.
Then it would be poles and baseball bats.
And then it would be knifes.
You'd be looking out the window going
Is that a wee boy with a sword?
Am I really seeing this?
And you and your granddad
You would just sit there and go
What are they fighting for?
Cos your grandda never went out and started hitting people.
He got his point across with his mouth, not with his hands.
He would just have to talk to you and people would listen to him.
And you'd remember you always wanted to grow up to be just like him.

Each new line is a new thought, a new memory, and each one is as electric and vivid as the last. They all join up to create a circuit board that illuminates how you come to be in the position you're in at the start of the play. It is an extraordinarily alive and detailed image. You may find it helpful to draw pictures as you imagine James's world, and the various members of your family, and the episodes you describe.

This is the beginning of the play. When you read the whole play, you'll realize that the piece is one long monologue, and you may choose to perform other sections of it, or even the whole thing. It can be performed by one actor or an ensemble.

Blooded

Isabel Wright

This play is set during the summer holidays after four girls have finished school. It is about their realization that their intense and extraordinary friendships are probably going to melt away as they enter their adult lives. They experience some dangerous, surprising and upsetting adventures during the long summer, and this speech is from one of them, known affectionately as FatB.

FatB   Mum always sent me to a pharmacy across town. Don't want folk knowing all our business she said. 'Don't want that lemonfaced cow round the corner knowing all our ins and outs'. Now I go all the way over there just to see him . . . Martin. In his sparkling white coat. His smile's sexy as hell. We gab away like anything. I feel like . . . I'm safe . . . like . . . I'm home. And it's not that way where your voice disappears down your throat and you squeak like Minnie mouse or something! I'm funny. And he's funny. And we're the same kind of funny. And it's like . . . all over my body . . . every single particle of me is alive or something! All of my skin and all of my hair and all of my arms and legs and fingers and toes are just waiting for him to touch me! And if he does I might explode! I might just explode! Cos if he does touch me, if I'm too busy gabbing to notice a car and I'm about to die or something, he'll pull me back and laugh and it's the best thing in the world! The best bloody thing in the world!

You're full of energy and excitement; it is the most exciting thing that has happened to you in your life. The important thing is to be in a state of worship about Martin. Let the audience decide what they think of him, all you can do is adore him. The first time you say his name out loud is momentous. The various sensations you describe should be enjoyed not only in your face, but should physically send tingles through your whole body.

Boat Memory

Laline Paull

*The boat referred to in the title of this play is The Beagle, on which
Charles Darwin sailed from Walthamstow in London to South America.
There he met three young people in Tierra del Fuego and brought them
back to England in 1830. Their presence in the community becomes
disruptive and leads to several traumatic events, which lead to the three
children being sent home.*

Hannah   Is everything still very strange, or have you been away from
. . . Tierra del Fuego . . . for so long now that strange is normal? (*on her
silence*) I've decided to talk to you as if you could understand everything
and then gradually you will – you'll be here three years, after all. And
when you go back you'll build a little church and show everyone how to
be a civilised Christian lady . . . hopefully. Am I talking too much?
People always say so. You can too if you want – we could have some sort
of signal, look, like this:

Hannah *puts her finger to her lips, shakes her head.* **Fuegia** *copies her.*
Hannah smiles.

You're a clever girl Captain FitzRoy said, and you look so to me. But a
clever girl is a waste, they say.

Hannah *sighs, pulls a white nightgown out from the white bedclothes.*
Fuegia *shrinks away.*

Miss Fuegia Basket, you cannot sleep in those funny clothes you wear.
Come now, it is I who should be more frightened of you, with all this talk
of cannibals. I have read Robinson Crusoe you know, from cover to
cover. Reverend disapproves of Mr Defoe, but Matthew lent it to me,
when we were . . . younger. Mr Matthew Wilson Esquire. *(holds up
nightgown again)* Come Miss Basket, please do not oblige me to change
you myself, you are a large grown girl – and look at it, a missionary
society sent it for you: it is absolutely new!

But **Fuegia** *shrinks away miserably, lies down on the ground and curls up.*

I know that you have slept in beds since you arrived, even though you
were used to hovels before. Reverend will be very displeased with me if
I cannot get you even to sleep, so come now:

Holding out the nightdress, **Hannah** *gets up purposefully.* **Fuegia**
cringes from her. **Hannah** *loses patience, gets into her own bed.*

Then be a savage and sleep on the ground like a dog, if that is what you
want. (*a beat*) Fuegia that floor is very cold, I'm telling you, you will get
sick if you lie there like that uncovered. Is that what you want, to get
sick? I don't want to nurse you either, I've got enough to do.

*Hannah is a fourteen-year-old parish girl in Walthamstow. She has been
brought up with a very strict and certain set of values and expectations.
When you play this speech, you might be able to find a friend to play the
silent part of the Fuegian girl, so you have someone to direct your
speech to, and someone who could respond to you physically.*

Broken Hallelujah

Sharman Macdonald

*This play explores the horrors of war and is set at the Siege of
Petersburg during the American Civil War. It is about a small group of
Union soldiers who are cooking stolen bacon and are discovered by two
girls from the South. Rowatt is one of the soldiers from the South and in
this scene he's explaining his views to two soldiers from the North in
their camp.*

Rowatt   You're in my land. I am not in yours.
   The way I see it. Leaving aside the question of all men being
   created equal for those better qualified than I am to argue,
   there's no viability to slavery in the South. It's run out of its
   viability. A man works to better his life, his and his family's.
   Else why would he work?
   Slave's life doesn't get any better no matter how hard he works. So he
      does as little as possible, eats as much as he can. Same as you or
      me would do in his position.
   He's not stupid, your slave. Low output, high maintenance. Doesn't
      make
   sense. So I'm not fighting for slavery – to keep slavery in the
   south – I'm not fighting for that.
   You dictate to us though.
   Righteously. Then you come here.
   You don't just fight. You burn and you steal. Unarmed women and
   children you pull their homes down round them. And I don't see by
   what right you do that.

*Read as much as you can about the American Civil War so you can begin
to understand what Rowatt's background might be and how that informs
his views. You should also listen to southern American accents online
and see if you can perform the speech in the accent of the character.*

Burn

Deborah Gearing

This play is about what happened to a fifteen-year-old in foster care on a hot summer's night by a river. The young man's name is Joey, but he is known as Birdman – he flies from nest to nest and has no family and no friends; he is a loner with nothing to lose. One lazy afternoon by the riverbank, the friends he never had narrate the story of his last dramatic day. One of the main characters who features in the story of his disappearance is Rachel.

Rachel   It was after eight when I saw Birdman.
  How I know –
  It's a bit complicated – I'll start at the beginning.
  Me sitting listening for Col –
  He's always late –
  Sitting listening to that little gold clock on the mantelshelf.
  It chimes on the half hour – just once
  Then on the full hour it does the whole works –
  Me sitting listening to it chime eight times –
  he's late he's late he's late he's late.
  Me sitting listening on the edge of my seat –
  I can't sit back because I'll put creases in my top.
  At eight he's late.
  Well late.
  I'm beginning to think he's gone off with someone else
  Mel or Linda or Jackie or Marie – they'd all go with him –
  he's only got to whistle.
  That's a line from a film, but he meant it nice.
  I mean – they're dogs – and they're nothing to him.

  I'm beginning to think I'll chuck that little gold clock out the window
  I'm beginning to think I'm not feeling too good –
  I'm beginning to shrink on the inside, and my mouth's all dry.
  Then the doorbell rings.

(*doorbell*)

  that's him
  And in a minute we're gonna go out

And in a minute we're gonna kiss
And in a minute we're gonna get all loved up
Hang on a minute Col. I just need to get my shoes.

Rachel is describing her personal situation on the evening when the main event of the play happened, the evening that Birdman burned-off in Colin's car. This speech comes at the beginning of the scene; it is as if the real-time action of the play freezes for a few minutes allowing Rachel to tell us how she was feeling the night that Birdman disappeared. She explains in detail that she was at home waiting for Colin to pick her up in the car as they had arranged to go out on a date. Deborah Gearing's play, like its title, is full of sounds and words that summon the senses. You should relish the sounds the words make in this speech. Notice how many letter 't's there are: what is the effect of the repetition of this consonant? Is it like the ticking clock on the mantelshelf? How can you use the repeated sound in your voice to complement the atmosphere the speech creates? This is a speech about anticipation. Think about how you can use the sounds in the speech to echo and mirror the sounds that Rachel describes, the ticking clock for example. Why do you think some of the lines begin with the same phrase? And what effect can this have on the listener?

Burying Your Brother in the Pavement

Jack Thorne

The play takes place on the pavement of a housing estate in a deprived suburban area. The main character is Tom, who is grieving for his brother Luke who has been murdered on the street. Tom spends the play campaigning to have his brother's body buried in the pavement where he died. The play is largely a series of flashbacks that illustrate the events leading up to his brother's death. This speech comes at the very end of the play.

Tom   The night he died – they basically forgot about me. Courtney said she heard Mum crying, and woke then, and came downstairs to find out. But I didn't hear anything. He hadn't come home, I knew that before I went to bed, but I figured he was just with mates, even Mum wasn't worried, so I slept well and slept deep. Anyway, about 4am. I woke up and I needed a piss, and a glass of milk, so I went downstairs. And Mum was in tears and sitting in a corner of the kitchen on the floor and Courtney was standing crying and Dad was just really really angry – saying things like 'well, what the hell was he doing down there'. And there was a police officer making everyone tea and trying to look unobtrusive and I – was – seeing all this was like – I just – and I didn't know what had happened.

Anyway, so I ask 'what's going on' and they all turn and look at me – and they didn't want to explain it all again – my parents didn't – so the police officer said – because she knew they didn't want to explain it again 'I'll take him in the living room, shall I? Let him know what's happening'. And Mum just nodded.

They'd told Courtney themselves, but that was probably because they knew she'd have a better reaction than me, and they wanted to hug her and stuff. I was never the sort of boy that people hugged, Luke was that sort of boy, I was – I'm the sort of boy people pat. On the back, head, or arm . . . Anyway, when the police officer told me and I asked 'are you sure' and she said 'that's a strange response' and I said nothing and that I probably needed to go to my room for a bit and she said OK and then I went and sat in my room and played solitaire on my computer. And –

He's not going to be buried here. They've put him in the ground already. They're hardly going to dig up the body to put in a concrete hole. But this is – my burial isn't it? The time I'm burying him, for me. And I know him now, and I know what I'm burying and I know what he means to me now, I know that I love him.

You know that don't you? I love you. You know that? And I'm sorry. I'm so sorry.

You have spent the whole play learning, bit by bit, the reasons why your brother died. Your speech at the end is full of regret, guilt and the early stages of grief. It should be filled with the extraordinary weight of all three.

Can You Keep a Secret?

Winsome Pinnock

*This is a realistic drama about a racially-motivated murder that takes
place in an urban working-class setting. A young black man called Derek
is murdered by a young white man called Sean. Derek's girlfriend,
Aleysha, struggles with grief and Sean's girlfriend, Kate, struggles with
the fact that she witnessed the murder – she can't get the images of what
happened out of her head. In this scene, a character who is known as
Weirdboy speaks to Kate, who remains silent throughout the speech.*

Weirdboy I'm so chuffed that we've become friends, Kate. It's what
I've always wanted. I've been on my own for such a long time. You
don't know how lonely I've been. And you're such a good listener.

What shall we do today? What do you fancy? A walk along the river?
Pictures? There's a couple of good films on I'd like to see. What about
you? We could eat something. I'll treat you. Anything you want. Not that
I've got much money on me. Or we could go shopping. You haven't been
shopping for a while. Haven't bought yourself a new outfit for ages.

Go on, Katie – you don't mind me calling you Katie do you? – treat
yourself. You mustn't let yourself go. What will Sean think if you don't
look good for him? I'll help you choose shall I?

Do you ever wonder what it would be like to be old, Katie? I do
sometimes. My aunt says I have an old soul. Which means that I'll
probably be happier when I'm older because by then I'll have caught up
with meself. Then it won't matter so much to belong to a group. Have
you noticed that about older people, Katie? They don't seem to want to
go around in packs. The older you get, the more you want to hide away
inside. That's why people marry I suppose. Do you think you and Sean
will marry?

Katie. I hope you don't mind me saying this but I don't think he's right
for you. When you're with him I get this sense that you're trying too
hard, do you know what I mean? That you're trying to be someone else.
It's no good if you can't be yourself with a man, Katie. One day the
game'll be up and the whole trick will fall apart won't it? Maybe it
already has. I mean, look at you Katie. I have to say it's something that's

always puzzled me: why is it that women love guys like Sean. What is it? My aunt says it's the challenge of the chase.

Did you know that I live with my aunt, Katie? It was either that or go into a home. You didn't know that did you? There's a lot about me that you probably don't know, isn't there? But now that we're friends, maybe we'll get to know each other better.

I've told her all about you. I told her that you didn't want to have anything to do with me and she said that I should just give it time, that you'd come round. And you have, haven't you?

Tired Kate? Why don't you just lie down and relax in the sun. You should relax more Katie. You always seem to be rushing off somewhere. What's the hurry? We've got all the time in the world.

He reaches over and strokes her face.

What's the matter Katie? I'm not that repulsive am I? What, can't I even touch you?

You're not too good for me, Katie. Do you think I don't know that? Remember, I know you Katie. I know everything that you are, everything you've done. You forget that I can read your mind. No, you can't put a wall up against me now. I can see everything and you know what I see, Katie? I see blood. I see death Katie, a young man dying and you killed him. You think you can hide in your silence Katie, but you can't hide from me. I know what you are. You're a murderer, Katie. A murderer.

Although you're known as Weirdboy because your background is different from the other kids', you're a young man who speaks a lot of sense and cuts through to the truth of what Kate is thinking, even though your language and actions towards her can, at times, be inappropriate and, at best, unhelpful. You need to think very carefully and in some detail about the reasons why you might have ended up with the slightly unusual qualities of character you have – in other words, as you fill out the back-story to the character you create, make each strange tic a manifestation or result of a sequence of real events, rather than merely making yourself weird.

Chatroom

Enda Walsh

*Virtually all of this play takes place in internet chatrooms. At first,
they're fairly light-hearted places where Harry Potter and Britney
Spears are discussed, but then the atmosphere darkens, and a small
group of young people persuade a boy who is suffering from depression
to commit suicide. The boy's name is Jim, and this is the speech in which
he explains to the compassionate girl, Eva, what happened on the day his
father left him.*

Jim Right well I'm six years old and my three brothers are going away
with my mother for the weekend . . . a treat for something or other. My
dad's staying behind and my mother says that he's to look after me. That
it would be a chance for us to bond. So they're gone and me and my dad
are sat at the kitchen table looking at each other. Like we're looking at
each other for the first time, you know. He asks me what I want to do and
straight away I say I want to go and see the penguins in the Zoo. When I
was six I was going through some mad penguin obsession. I used to
dress up as a penguin at dinner times and always ask for fish fingers . . .
stuff like that. If it wasn't penguins it was cowboys. Cowboys were cool.
A penguin dressed as a cowboy was always a step too far funnily
enough!

So we go to the Zoo and I wear my cowboy outfit . . . get my gun and
holster, my hat and all that. We get the bus and it's sort of funny to see
my dad on the bus and away from the house. We start to have this chat
about when I was born and what a really fat baby I was . . . but how after
a day or so I stopped eating any food and everyone was dead worried.
That *he* was very worried. That he was so happy when I got better and
they could take me home. (*slight pause*) We're in the Zoo and I go
straight to the penguins. Standing in my cowboy gear . . . looking at the
penguins . . . having such a great chat to my dad on the bus . . . it was a
perfect childhood day. (*slight pause*) He lets go of my hand and says
he'll be back with my choc ice. And he goes. (*pause*) He's gone. (*pause*)
I'm happy looking at the penguins but it's an hour since he's left and I go
to look for him. I'm walkin' about the Zoo and I'm not worried yet. And
I don't talk to anyone. I leave the Zoo and I go to the bus stop we got off
at earlier. I get on the bus. I tell the driver my address. He asks where my

parents are and I say they're at home waiting for me. I stay on the bus in the seat nearest the driver. After a while we end up at the end of our street and the driver says, 'So long cowboy'. (*laughs a little*) He was nice. (*pause*) I get the key from under the mat and open the door and go inside the house. And I'm alone there and I suppose I still think my dad will be coming back soon. I take off my cowboy clothes and hang up my hat and holster. It being Saturday night I have a bath and get into my pyjamas because my dad would have liked that. I have a glass of milk and some biscuits and watch 'Stars In Their Eyes' 'cause that was his favourite programme on the telly. (*slight pause*) It's getting dark outside and I start to worry. The house is feeling too big so I get my quilt and take it into the bathroom and lock the bathroom door and it feels safer with the door locked so I stay in there. And he's not coming back. (*pause*) He's never coming back.

This is a speech in which you slowly but surely reveal to Eva, and indeed yourself, the awful horror that your father has abandoned you. Notice that you begin by describing all that was pleasant and enjoyable about your life on the day before you realized your father has disappeared. This build-up enables you to paint a happy picture that we then visualize turning bleak as you reveal the story of what happened.

Children of Killers

Katori Hall

Set fifteen years after the Rwandan genocide, Children of Killers *follows
a group of teenage friends as their fathers are being released from prison
where they have been serving time for their roles in the mass killings of
their Tutsi neighbours. The play asks how the innocent children, who are
too young to remember their fathers, are going to live ordinary lives with
such a brutal legacy. The play contains scenes that are naturalistically
set in domestic environments, and also atmospheric and expressionistic
settings; this speech is one of the latter. We see Esperance, a young girl
who has lost an arm in the genocide, carrying a basket of purple flowers
and sprinkling them on a patch of grass by the roadside. As she speaks,
the ghosts of young girls who have lost their lives come and lay their
hands upon her. She is dreading the release of the prisoners.*

Esperance   You told me that this day would never come. You promised
me. When you were in the hospice you said that the worst was over.
'Don't worry, I am the last victim of the genocide.' I remember you
saying. 'I am the last.' You hear that song? That sweet song that rings of
murder? They are coming home. They are coming home to finish what
they started. They can kill you fast, or they can kill you slow, but at the
end of the day they still kill you. They killed you slowly. So slowly. I
don't know why you wouldn't tell me. I knew. I knew you had the
sickness, mama. I knew you took those pills. But then you got worse.
You got worse, mama. Who knew that Death would take so long, toying
with you, torturing you? You would have thought the rape would be
enough, but Death came right along to screw you until your dying day.
Filling your lungs until you could not breathe. Ripping your skin with
sores. Who knew one would rather die at the stroke of the machete than
of the slow tick-tock of the AIDS clock. Our little Emmanuel is . . .
getting worse. We try to get the money together every month, you know,
for his medicine . . . he's selling credit in the streets, I'm weaving baskets
and selling them by the roadside, it's barely enough . . . I don't know
what I'll do without him. If he goes then . . . what am I going to do? I'll
be the only one left. The only one left of our family. They are singing in
the streets. In the cabarets. They are coming home. My neighbors, my
killers . . . I feel like I'm back beneath the dead bodies again. I'm back to
being smothered beneath the weight of the dead. When they found me,

they thought I was gone. Blood, blood everywhere. Somehow I survived, but mama, I'm tired. I don't think I can be a survivor anymore.

You're talking to your mother. We assume you're sprinkling the purple flowers onto a patch of grass where either your mother is buried or where she lost her life. The crucial thing with this speech is that you play it as if you are actually talking to your mother; as if you were sitting in an everyday place, like the kitchen of your home. If you overemphasize the high-stakes emotional context of what you have to say to your mother, it won't be believable.

You are in a state of acute trauma but what you have to do to continue with the next part of your day is to find a solace and strength by imagining that your mother is still alive and that you can share your anxiety with her – it's therapeutic. If you play this speech as relentless bad news, it won't be dramatically interesting.

The Chrysalids

David Harrower, based on the novel by John Wyndham

*This play is set in a place called Waknuk, where there is a distinction
between two types of people: the 'mutants' and the 'pures'. A group
of young pures discover they have telepathic powers and realize
that this makes them mutants. They must escape to the fringes,
where they discover that the mutants are less different than they
thought.*

Michael I knew them better than my brother and sister
    five others who shared this double life
    inhabitants of a secret world
    that was thrilling at first
    with a language that was ours alone
    where no one corrected or punished us
    for expressing what we felt
    Then as the wall got higher, I turned away
    the shouts for purity louder
    each of us turned away
    slowly descending the world we'd made
    going back to ourselves and our families
    becoming alone again.
    until Petra . . .
    came dazzling like sunlight
    her thoughts chaotic, overpowering
    drawing us all to her, together again
    as she learned our language
    as we taught her how to share her thoughts
    as we returned to the world we'd lost.

*Read the novel as well as the play. You are one of the telepathic children.
You have very special powers. Think carefully about the way the
playwright has laid out the words on the page, how the speech is
structured – each line suggests a new thought. Work through the speech
and make a note of what you think each new thought might be.*

You should also work through the speech line by line, picturing each of the strong images that are described and imagine ways you can project those images through the quality of your voice.

Citizenship

Mark Ravenhill

This is an odyssey about a schoolboy called Tom who is trying to decide who he'd most like to go out with, a boy or a girl. He tries sleeping with a girl, and she becomes pregnant. This speech is given by the baby she gives birth to.

Baby   And so it happened. My mummy and my daddy made me that night.

Neither of them enjoyed it very much. But they did it. And that's what they wanted. And that night I started to grow in my mummy's tummy. And by the time she did her GCSEs I was almost ready to come out of her tummy.

I think that night as they lay together in the dark she thought they might spend all their time together from that day on. But that didn't happen. In fact, once that night was over, they were sort of shy and embarrassed whenever they saw each other until – by the time I was born – they weren't speaking to each other at all. But mummy says for a few moments – she's sure there were a few moments that night when he did really, really love her. And I believe her.

Most of this play is fairly naturalistic, apart from a couple of moments, and this is one of them. The baby exists without a calendar age. You need to make some choices about how you play him or her; is the speech comic, sad or a combination of both?

Cloud Busting

Helen Blakeman

This is the story of Davey and how he was bullied in school because he had 'fizzy-feet'. He was a lively little boy who suffered from asthma. One day, through a careless accident, he had an attack that led to him going to hospital, because he couldn't get to his inhaler in time. The play is based on a poetic novel by Malorie Blackman, in which each chapter is a different type of poem.

Davey   What's more than nothing?
  Everything.
  Why do most kids listen to the same type of music?
  Cos they don't know any better.
  Music is food for the nerve endings.
  It makes you happy, it makes you sad.
  It makes you dance.
  Sometimes it makes your day.
  We don't all have the same kind of day.
  Why listen to the same kind of music?
  We'd all be so much happier that way.
  Our own tune.
  Our own signature.

You are thirteen years old. You're an extraordinary child. You have a more than usual optimistic outlook on life. When you look at the clouds in the sky you see pictures. When you move, you can't help but dance. When you see conflict, you can't compute it, it is inexplicable to you and it causes you much confusion.

Cuba

Liz Lochhead

*This play is set in a Scottish girls' school during the Cuban missile crisis
of 1962. Two of the girls, Barbara and Bernadette, make a protest by
spray-painting a slogan on the head teacher's door. Although they are
both punished for this act of vandalism they receive different forms of
punishment because they are from different social backgrounds. The play
has a narrator called B, who you realize is one of the girls in later adult
life. You don't discover until the end of the play whether B refers to
Barbara or Bernadette.*

B. That's never us. It is though! There she is, and there's me. Back row,
to the left. There we are. Barbara and Bernadette, Berni and Barb.
Unbelievable.

Palgrave's golden treasury . . . Every home should have one. I didn't
know we did . . . Not a lot of poetry round our house, not that I can
remember, not when I was growing up. Maybe I should take it back to
Sarah, little souvenir of your Grandma, mmm? Must've been Mum's . . .
Oh look, a school prize!

She was so proud of you Sairey, when you were born that was the first
thing I did she ever really approved of. You two always got on like a
house on fire. I know how much you're going to miss her. I'll miss her.
Oh mum, I miss you so much. Where are you?

Come on, come on, B. The sooner you get this done the sooner you can
go home. (*She picks up photograph.*) Take this? This'll make Will laugh.
Wonder if my lot would recognize me? Which one's Mum? Can you see
me? Which one am I? That's us, Bernadette and Barbara, Barbara and
Bernadette. Inseparable. Hah! So they said. So we thought. Thing is we
came from very different families.

*You should hold a photo as you perform this speech, and it would
probably help if it was a real photo of you and a friend when you
were younger. This will help you to enter the mindset of B as she*

remembers the naïveté of her early days at school. You should also decide which lines would be best spoken to the faces you can see in the photograph and which lines should be shared directly with the faces in the audience.

Dead End

Letizia Russo, translated by Aleks Sierz

This play is about a young man called Sirius who is God. A group of young people worship him, even though he continually makes mistakes. A couple called Kris and Kent arrive on the hill where Sirius lives and rules, and Kent claims to be the one true God. Trouble ensues. This is the speech where Kent tells Kris about his childhood while they're on the journey to Sirius's kingdom.

Kent Now I can tell you. I was eleven. I was born in the place where we're going to and I stayed there eleven years. But one day, when I was eleven, something happened. I forgot who I was. I couldn't remember anymore. I stayed outside the town. I stayed on a hill. With a railway nearby. It wasn't used anymore when I was there. I wasn't alone on the hill, there was him, my friend, the one we're going to meet. We played. We had a lot of laughs. And then I don't remember anything at all. I know I fell down. I always kept my eyes open. I never closed them. But I don't remember. The only thing I remember is him looking at me, with blood on him. He was looking at me as if I was dead. I had my eyes open, but I couldn't speak. I was half dead, but I felt better than him. I wanted to say something, but I couldn't. I don't know how long we stared at each other. Then he escaped. He shouted. He shouted so loudly and he was so scary, he looked almost happy. I stayed there for a while, then I left. And then I remembered who I was.

When you read the whole play, you'll discover that Dead End is set in a strange, invented world, which occasionally bears resemblance to the world we know. In this speech, you need to imagine the whole back-story of Kent, as well as creating an understanding of what your relationship with Kris is like, and why you're telling him this story. The crux of the story you are telling Kris is that the boy you are on your way to meet caused you to have an out of body experience. You are remembering a moment of great significance that shaped the rest of your life.

Dirty Dirty Princess

Georgia Fitch

This play starts with a rumour going around the neighbourhood that thirteen-year-old Stacey has had sex with an older teenage boy at a party. Although it isn't true, Stacey is distraught that she can't control the situation and that she can't make the rumour go away. She is also called a 'princess' by the other kids because her mother has a plasma television. In this speech, Billie, who is the boy's long term girlfriend, has grabbed Stacey by the hair and is torturing her in front of her gang.

Billie   He drinks too much drink innit and running and drink don't mix . . . and if he wants to go for Gold, then he has to stop that . . . I know that, his coach knows that and he knows that man . . . He gets early up to train and his body is then out of the flow like if he smokes and drinks . . . and then he makes bad choices . . . choices like you Princess . . . choices like . . . Just like Ashley did with Cheryl . . . just like Ashley Cole did to his . . . woman . . . remember?

(Billie *tightens her grip.)*

Seeing you about for years innit, little girl in ankle socks, tap dancing in the street, Mummy and Daddy's pride and joy . . . living in a plasma Buckingham Palace, clean windows, shiny front door with Daddy's BMW parked outside! Walking your dog, head to toe in yer Primark Pink, laughing with your friend and I HATE YOU . . . I HATE ALL GIRLS LIKE YOU, BUT I ESPECIALLY HATE GIRLS REALLY LIKE YOU BECAUSE INSIDE YOU IS HEARTLESS GAL, VERY VERY HEARTLESS, AND YOU CARE ABOUT NOBODY BUT YOUR SELF . . . It's the: *(acting and performing to her gang)* I am oh so lucky girl innit, the girl who has and takes everything she wants, never had anything bad happen to her in life, no tears or nightmares at bedtime for Princess . . . Cause you know the world belongs to you, THE PERFECT WORLD IS YOUR DOLLS HOUSE AND YOU ARRANGE THE FURNITURE JUST THE WAY YOU WANT and you can own any girl's action man yeah . . . Well little Barbie sket . . . Dirty Dirty Princess . . . Not so clean now innit?

(Billie *throws her to the ground and rubs* **Stacey**'*s face in the mud,*

Stacey *tries to wipe her face.)*

See you think you are so so special . . . but you are nothing, not worth a
text and just like us now . . . Some ho . . . some little thing that Daniel
was tricked by because he had too too much drink . . . some pink bitch
sket leading him on and . . . it meant nothing . . . and you meant nothing
to him see . . . SEE?

(*Performing even more to her gang, they smile back sheepishly.*)

I don't want to seriously hurt you or kill you even . . . cause I have bigger
fish to fry and Luke Palmer pleaded to go easy on you . . . but if you ever
sex up my man again . . . I will put you in hospital for a long LONG
time . . . you hear . . . YOU HEAR ME . . . Now go back to Barbie,
Mummy with all the shopping bags and Buckingham Palace and don't
walk these streets no more . . . I don't want to see you about . . . you get
me . . . You get me? (*beat*) You hear? (*big big beat*) You hear . . . .

*This is a very aggressive, physically demanding speech. Billie is a strong
force and totally dominates Stacey in the scene, and plays up to her gang
who are watching the situation in silence. When you play this speech,
you must imagine that you have another actress in your grip, and that
you are holding her in such a position that she can't get up off the ground
and escape the violence you are threatening her with. As you learn the
speech, choose where to vary it in terms of pace and pitch, it can't all be
full throttle!*

Discontented Winter: House Remix

Bryony Lavery

A riff on Richard III, this stylish poetic, rapping, musical play is about two princes and a group of posh Sloanie girls who kidnap them for mischief. It all takes place at night in a crazy landscape that is dominated by flash mobs and hoodlums. Ronan is head-hoodlum, and he opens the play with this speech.

Ronan Now's not a good time
  For why? For this
  Adults are arses
  Grown-ups gobshites
  Our Leaders lie
  Smell the wind whiffo!
  Something's came to an end
  Chaos kicked off
  Her boots broke my head
  The spinning world's been spun
  Its icy ends at boiling point
  near and far . . . we're frying tonight
  Phew! What a Scorcher
  And Me? . . . I'm Feeling
  hot hot hot
  look at me
  arrived too early out of a whore's fanny
  she dinks my unborn foetus
  with the blow the crack
  then drops me, disgraceful!
  one mad night
  on the floor of a Soho shite house
  and I grow up a spaz
  Dogs bark when I crip by them
  All This makes me Bitter
  Therefore
  I am decided to be the Bad Boy
  in this (*drips venom*) Youth Issues Play!

In this speech you are explaining to the audience why you are full of malice. You are able to be outside the story just for the first minutes of the play and to directly address the audience so they get a glimpse into your personal history, your back-story, what made you what you are.

Technically, really enjoy and savour the fantastic vowel sounds in the lines of the speech, and also the rhymes – see how many you can spot. Rhythm is everything here; as you learn the speech, experiment with as many different ways of doing it as you can. Make it your own.

DNA

Dennis Kelly

This play is about a group of friends who, while out playing in the woods, accidentally knock one of their classmates, Adam, down some sort of well. They cover up their crime so convincingly that an innocent man in the town is arrested and accused of murder. This double tragedy causes chaos among the group as they respond to the events in many different ways. One of the group, Leah, who wasn't directly involved in the incident, spends her days sitting next to her silent friend, Phil, in a field – she finds herself doing all the talking . . .

A Field. Leah and Phil, Phil eating an ice cream.

Leah   What are you thinking?

No answer.

No, don't tell me, sorry, that's a stupid, that's such a stupid—

You can tell me, you know. You can talk to me. I won't judge you, whatever it is. Whatever you're, you know, I won't, I won't . . .

Is it me?

Not that I'm—

I mean it wouldn't matter if you weren't or were, actually, so—

Are you thinking about me?

No answer.

What good things? Phil? Or . . .

I mean is it a negative, are you thinking a negative thing about—

Not that I'm bothered. I'm not bothered, Phil, I'm not, it doesn't, I don't care. You know. I don't . . .

What, like I talk too much? Is that it? That I talk too much, you, sitting there in absolute silence thinking 'Leah talks too much, I wish she'd shut up once in a while' is that it, is that what you're, because don't, you know, judge, you know, because alright, I do. There, I'm admitting, I am admitting, I talk too much, so shoot me. So kill me, Phil, call the police, lock me up, rip out my teeth with a pair of rusty pliers, I talk too much, what a crime, what a sin, what an absolute catastrophe, stupid, evil, ridiculous, because you're not perfect actually, Phil. Okay? There. I've said it, you're not . . .

You're a bit . . .

You're . . .

Pause. She sits.

Do I disgust you? I do. No, I do. No don't because, it's alright, it's fine, I'm not gonna, you know, or whatever, you know it's not the collapse of my, because I do have, I could walk out of here, there are friends, I've got, I've got friends, I mean alright, I haven't got friends, not exactly, I haven't, but I could, if I wanted, if I wanted, given the right, given the perfect, you know, circumstances. So don't, because you haven't either, I mean it's not like you're, you know, Mr, you know, popular, you know, you haven't, you know, you haven't, you know, you haven't, but that's, that's different, isn't it, I mean it is, it is, don't say it isn't, really, don't, you'll just embarrass us both because it is different, it's different because it doesn't matter to you. Does it. Sitting there. Sitting there, all . . .

all . . .

You're not scared. Nothing scares, there, I've said it; scared. Scared, Phil. I'm scared, they scare me, this place, everyone, the fear, the fear that everyone here, and I'm not the only one, I'm not the only one, Phil, I'm just the only one saying it, the fear that everyone here lives in, the brutal terror, it scares me, okay, I've said it and I am not ashamed. Yes, I am ashamed but I'm not ashamed of my shame, Phil, give me that much credit at least, thank you.

Everyone's scared.

S'not just me.

Pause.

We've got each other.

We need each other.

So don't give it all . . .

You need me as much as . . .

Don't give it all the . . .

Beat.

What are you thinking?

*You should give the impression that you're talking to the
ever-silent Phil, who you adore even though he is impossible to read and
he rarely acknowledges what you say. You should give
the impression that you're trying to get through to him, but also find a
way of opening the speech out to the audience so that we
see that your questions are reaching out to the whole universe.
You have a quick, inquisitive mind, and each question should be asked
in a way that is distinct from the last, yet shares the same guarded
urgency.*

*At the end of the play, Leah is gone and Phil sits alone in the field where
they used to spend time together. Richard comes to visit him.*

Richard   Phil, Phil, watch this! Phil, watch me, watch me, Phil!

He walks on his hands.

See? See what I'm doing? Can you see, Phil?

He collapses. **Phil** *doesn't even look at him.*

Richard *gets up, brushes himself down, and sits with* **Phil.**

Silence.

When are you going to come back?

Phil *shrugs?*

Come on, Phil. Come back to us. What do you want to sit up here for? In
this field? Don't you get bored? Don't you get bored sitting here, every
day, doing nothing?

No answer.

Everyone's asking after you. You know that? Everyone's saying 'where's
Phil?' 'what's Phil up to?' 'when's Phil going to come down from that
stupid field?' 'wasn't it good when Phil was running the show?' What do
you think about that? What do you think about everyone asking after you?

No answer.

Aren't you interested? Aren't you interested in what's going on?

No answer.

John Tate's found god. Yeah, Yeah I know. He's joined the Jesus Army, he runs round the shopping centre singing and trying to give people leaflets. Danny's doing work experience at a dentist's. He hates it. Can't stand the cavities, he says when they open their mouths sometimes it feels like you're going to fall in.

Pause.

Brian's on stronger and stronger medication. They caught him staring at a wall and drooling last week. It's either drooling or giggling. Keeps talking about earth. I think they're going to section him. Cathy doesn't care. She's too busy running things. You wouldn't believe how thing's have got, Phil. She's insane. She cut some kid's finger off, that's what they say anyway.

Doesn't that bother you? Aren't you even bothered?

No answer.

Lou's her best friend, now. Dangerous game. I feel sorry for Lou. And Jan and Mark have taken up shoplifting, they're really good at it, get you anything you want.

Phil?

Phil!

He shakes **Phil** *by the shoulders. Slowly* **Phil** *looks at him.*

You can't stay here forever. When are you going to come down?

Phil *says nothing.* **Richard** *lets go.*

Phil *goes back to staring at nothing.*

Pause.

Nice up here.

As I was coming up here there was this big wind of fluff. You know, this big wind of fluff, like dandelions, but smaller, and tons of them, like fluffs of wool or cotton, it was really weird, I mean it just came out of nowhere, this big wind of fluff, and for a minute I thought I was in a cloud, Phil. Imagine that. Imagine being inside a cloud, but with space inside it as well, for a second, as I was coming up here I felt like I was an alien in a cloud. But really felt it. And in that second, Phil, I knew that there was life on other planets. I knew we weren't alone in the universe, I didn't just think it or feel it, I knew it, I know it, it was as if the universe was suddenly shifting and giving me a glimpse, this vision that could see everything, just for a fraction of a heartbeat of a second. But I couldn't see who they were or what they were doing or how they were living.

How do you think they're living, Phil?

How do you think they're living?

No answer.

There are more stars in the universe than grains of sand on Brighton beach.

Pause.

Come back, Phil.

Phil?

No answer. They sit in silence.

Richard is a naturally optimistic person and a natural leader. He is the one who can always see a chink of light at the end of a seemingly endless tunnel. Phil has reached a point in his life where he can't see the point in carrying on; Richard describes, profoundly, the great joy to be found in being alive.

Dust

Sarah Daniels

This play begins on a Tube train, which is evacuated when an unattended bag is discovered. One of the girls, Flavia, is on a school trip and decides to stay behind in the carriage because she wants to escape her bullying classmates. She gets off at a disused platform and discovers she has travelled back in time to Roman London where a female gladiator takes her under her guardianship. In the huge empire in which Flavia finds herself, she meets many unusual characters who bear similarities to her unruly classmates. The woman who gives this speech is a woman who used to be carrying a baby, but is not anymore.

Woman with Baby   I was the girl whose panties stank of poverty, who grew to be a woman who smelt of stale breast milk, who gave birth then turned her face to the wall, who gave her baby away, whose kid died for lack of food, out of neglect, who used her dead baby to smuggle drugs, who abandoned her child on the train to Auschwitz, who murdered her offspring in a fit of jealous rage at its innocent lack of anxiety.

You look at me like I'm the shit on your shoes but you cannot shake my dust from your feet. You've drawn me into your lungs but you want to suffocate me coz I'm now part of you. I have always been with you.

You have always revelled in reviling me but you have no room to breathe because after two thousand years of your civilisation I am still alive and thriving amongst you and you are more concerned with making sure animals don't become extinct than with trying to eradicate me.

There is determination, anger and rage in this speech. When you have read the whole play and understood how the playwright has created the characters that emerge in the Roman Empire, you'll begin to see how to create the character who gives this speech. There is a fantastical combination of epic and personal here; you need to be able to communicate the two simultaneously. You should also relish the alliterative play within the lines, which will enable you to make the statements even more emphatically.

Eclipse

Simon Armitage

*This play is written by a poet, is mainly in verse and is about an incident
which takes place on a beach in Cornwall in 1999. A group of friends is
preparing to watch the total eclipse of the sun when a strange girl
approaches them and then disappears during the minutes of darkness.
The story is presented in alternating scenes of the characters giving their
account of events at a police station and in flashbacks to the day of the
eclipse.*

Tulip   When she left us for good I was nine or ten. Ran off with the
milkman, so
>
> Dad said. Ran off with the man in the moon, as far as I care. Grew up
> with
>
> uncles, cousins, played rugby football, swapped a pram for a ten-
> speed
>
> drop-handlebar, played with matches instead, flags and cars, threw the
> dolls
>
> on a skip and the skates on a dustcart, flogged the frills and pink stuff
> at a
>
> car-boot sale, burnt the Girl Guide outfit in the back garden, got kitted
> out
>
> at Famous Army Stores and Top Man. And Oxfam. I'll tell you
> something
>
> that sums it up; found a doll's house going mouldy in the attic –
> boarded it
>
> up, kept a brown rat in it. Put it all behind now, growing out of it, Dad
> says,
>
> says I'm blossoming, and I suppose he must be right. Klondike? No,
> not a
>
> boyfriend, more like a kid brother, really, known him since as far back
> as I
>
> can remember. Kissed him? Who wants to know? I mean, no, sir,
> except on
>
> his head, just once, on his birthday. Him and Lucy? Well, she took a
> shine to
>
> him, he told her some things and I think, she liked him. She just
> showed up

and wanted to tag along, make some friends, I suppose, mess about, have
fun; she had a few tricks up her sleeve, wanted . . . alright, if you put it like
that . . . to be one of the group. It's not much cop being on your own. Which
was fine by us. It's not that we gave it a second thought, to tell you the
truth. She just turned up that afternoon like a lost dog. She was one of the
gang. Then she was gone.

Tulip is describing the mysterious girl who has disappeared on the beach. Throughout the play, the six suspects are interviewed one at a time by an unseen police officer. They stare straight out at the audience as if they're being questioned. In the scenes between these monologues we see the events on the beach being played out. When learning this speech and researching the character within the context of the whole play, ask yourself what your attitude towards Lucy Lime is. Do you like her? In what ways are you different? How might this emerge in the speech? How does your childhood influence how you relate to the other teenagers around you in the play?

Midnight   Martin Blackwood, they call me Midnight –
it's a sick joke but I don't mind. Coffee
please, two sugars, white – don't ask me
to say that I saw, I'm profoundly blind,
but I'll tell you as much as I can, all right?

Cornwall, August, as you know. There's a beach
down there, seaside and all that, cliffs with caves
at the back, but up on the hill there's a view
looking south, perfect for watching a total eclipse
of the sun. The mums and dads were up on the top,
we were down in the drop – we'd just gone along
for the trip, killing a few hours. You see
it's like watching birds or trains but with planets
and stars, and about as much fun as cricket
in my condition, or 3D. There was Glue Boy,

Polly and Jane, Tulip and Klondike and me.
Thing is, we were messing around in the caverns
when Lucy appeared. Her mother and father
were up with the rest of the spotters; she wasn't
from round here. Thing is, I was different then,
did a lot of praying, wore a cross, went to church,
thought I was walking towards the light of the Lord –
when it's as dark as it is in here, you follow
any road with any torch. Lucy put me on the straight
and narrow. There's no such thing as the soul,
there's bone and there's marrow. It's just biology.
You make your own light, follow your own nose.
She came and she went. And that's as much as I know.

*You are a profoundly blind suspect, one of the group of young people
being interviewed by the police about the disappearance of Lucy Lime
during the eclipse. We never find out precisely what you had to do with
the incident, or indeed, what you really know or don't know about what
went on; the whole episode is shrouded in mystery. You must play each
segment of the speech with specific and precise intention; that way you
will fox all listeners as to what it is you're really about. The audience
never sees the detective – the audience is the detective; that is part of the
conceit of these monologues in the play – therefore you have full
permission to visually use the audience as listener, in the way you deliver
the speech, even though you cannot actually see them.*

The Edelweiss Pirates

Ayub Khan Din

This play is based on true events surrounding a group of young insurgents inside the Nazi Youth movement who rebelled against the Third Reich by causing trouble from within. It is set in Cologne, Germany, in the 1930s and 40s, and in this speech, one of the main characters, Klaus, is explaining what happened to his parents.

Klaus Becker   My parents were political. I grew up with politics. They were communists. They were always out on the streets demonstrating against the Nazis. All my life, all I ever remember are smoky rooms full of people talking and arguing politics. How to bring about the revolution, then, how to combat the Nazis . . . And then . . . then it all went quiet, no more open talk or Russia or comrade Stalin. Suddenly, our world was whispered and shadowed . . . hidden. The worry of my parents every time there was a knock on the door. It's as if we were waiting for them to come. They were always expected, anticipated. Then one day they did come. I was playing with my friend across the hall. The boots came up the stairs, I saw them coming. Climbing up. The black boots. Shiny boots. They stopped outside our apartment and knocked. I knew inside the apartment, my parents would have turned to the door instantly, knew, they would have turned to each other. Knew my father's look would have told my mother not to worry. His always, reassuring look. But not this time . . . I saw the door open . . . heard my mother screaming, my father on the floor, blood pouring from his nose and mouth, as the shiny boots rained down on his face and body. My mother, as she is dragged along the hall by her hair, screaming. My father looked at me as he passed and even through the blood and the pain, the look . . . he gave me the reassuring look . . . the look of my father, the look that said, all would be well . . .
I never saw them again.
They were both shot in Dachau.

You'll find this speech has three parts: in the first third you provide the audience with a picture of the landscape of your childhood; in the second part you start to focus on a particular time-frame; in the third and harrowing part, you explain specifically what you remember happening when you saw your parents taken away by the Nazis.

Follow, Follow

Katie Douglas

This play is set on the west coast of Scotland during an Orange Order march. In a quiet part of some woodland, there's an open patch of grass where eight teenagers are sitting drinking as it grows dark. Billy is one of them, he's sixteen and he's been waiting for his dad to turn up.

Billy   People don't always do what they say they're gonna do. I know that. I mean he's rung up before. Said – said he wanted to see me. That he missed me. Once, he invited me round to his. He's got this massive new house up in the next town. Four beds or whatever. And he rung me up all like, come over. Have your dinner with us. Us meaning him and his new wife. The new kids. So I went. I stole money out my Mum's purse for the bus fare cos she hates him, she'd never have loaned me it, and I got on the bus and I went. I got there and – house was dark. No car in the drive, blinds all pulled. I'm like, what's going on? Worried, y'know. Emergency or something maybe. My phone was out of credit so I sat on the front step and waited. Biting cold. Freezing, it was. Dunno how long I waited. Eventually they turned up, boot full of Tesco shopping. The wife's looks at me like she's trod in something. Like there's a bad smell in the air. And he's like full of apologies. Slipped my mind. Something came up. Busy lives. Another time?

Another time. Turn on my heel and go and I'm waiting for him to call me back. Check on me. How you getting home? Need a lift?

He keeps schtum. I keep walking. Last bus has gone so . . . kipped down in the shelter. After a while – you don't even feel the cold.

I know it's daft. I know cos when he was with us he was this useless bag of shit and now he's all sorted and has this life that means he gets to look down on us and I should tell him where to go, I know I should but—

But the phone rings and I can't help it. A bit of me always believes. This time, this time, this time.

Your dad is an alcoholic and although he's now more settled with his new wife, he often lets you down. You live in hope that he'll take more interest in your life. You'll notice that this speech is written in a Scottish accent but there's no reason why you can't perform this speech in any accent – Billy's story will ring true anywhere.

Frank & Ferdinand

Samuel Adamson

This play is based on the many versions of the Pied Piper story, which has its origins in medieval Germany. One hundred and thirty children have vanished overnight in a country that is at war; four children have been left behind. Their accounts of what happened during the night differ slightly and they each speak of a mysterious character called Sebastian who has clearly entered all their lives. The play explores what is real and what is imaginary. This speech concludes the play and is spoken by Flora, who has been silent until this point.

Flora Once upon a time, a certain village was overrun with rats, and a mysterious man appeared, wearing a scarf, or was it a coat, of several colours, and he claimed to be a rat-catcher, and he promised that for a certain sum he would rid the town of the rats. And the Mayor agreed, and from his pocket the boy, that is man, produced a recorder, or perhaps a pipe, I don't remember, and when he played the rats followed him into the river, where they drowned. Now rat-free, the Mayor of the town, or city, in New Zealand, or Palestine, or was it China, decided not to pay the Piper, and the Piper left angry, but on the twenty-sixth of June, or twenty-second of July, you decide, he returned, now dressed even more colourfully, with a lurid cummerbund, or was it scarf, or a white feather in his hat or moreover a black-and-white feather, which caused him to be called pied. And he played his pipe, and this time children followed and disappeared into a cave in the flattened hills that used to exist where the church now stands, that's the truth, ask the elders.

Beat.

One hundred-and-twenty nine children were lost that day or was it night, though some say some were left behind. They say a blind girl was not able to show where they went but that she'd heard a violin, or recorder, or pipe. A lame boy was not able to say where they'd gone as he couldn't keep up, and some say to compensate he told lies that bred like so many mice. A shy boy claimed he knew where they went, because he went half-way, but his timidity had made him scared of the hills, so he came back for a torch, or was it his coat, and by the time he'd got it, they'd vanished, and when the Mayor and parents pressed him for the truth, the shy boy dithered and ummed so much they tired of him.

A mute girl saw everything, but as she was mute and illiterate, her story went with her to her grave.

A gunshot. **Flora** *doesn't move or react, except to put a hand to her chest. As she removes it, blood is there.*

And the moral is don't talk to strangers, keep promises and pay your debts, and many cheerful songs have been written to memorialise the lost children, and the village is now pure and happy and somewhat rich and even tourists on visitors passes come to see the cave which has been constructed at the end of the High Street, and they recite the poems and sing the songs and watch the plays and photograph the statue outside the delicious bakery of the colourful piper smiling his come-hither smile, the end.

This is pure storytelling: you can decide how you want to characterize Flora and what tone you'd like to take. You could be magical and mysterious or very matter of fact, or a combination of the two. The essential thing is to be clear. In the final section of the speech, we realize that you are speaking to us, the audience, from beyond the grave.

Friendly Fire

Peter Gill

*A group of young people meet in the evenings by the war memorial in
their small town. We discover that three of them are trapped in a love
triangle which is ruining their friendship. The statue they meet by is of a
soldier dressed in First World War uniform, and it represents the
struggles of young men during the Great War. In the final scene, the
statue comes to life. This is Gary's speech, one of the people trapped in
the love triangle. He is talking to Adie.*

Gary I can't do nothing about nothing. Here or in the world. I like
being in control. I'm not in control of nothing. I want power. I want to
be in charge of nothing more like. We can do nothing. We know we
can't. I can't do nothing. What can we do?

I can't do anything. What can we do? You got no joy of doing anything.
Don't matter what I think. Don't matter, except for trainers. Except for
can I have a mountain bike, mum? You know, you're like that. No
choice. No choice.

I know what's going to happen. I know what's going to happen. Nothing.
Nowt. Turn you down. Failed. Not picked for the seven-a-side. We're left
out, let down. Impotent. Get it up where? Cold water. Drenched, pouring
down. I'm not kicking in. Fuck up. No marks. Doing my very best.
Could try harder. I'm not an individual. I don't want to be an individual.
Sometimes I'm me. Sometimes I'm you. Sometimes I'm from our street.
Sometimes I'm in the pictures. Sometimes, sometimes, I don't know
what they want, sometimes, sometimes I'm a prisoner. Sometimes I'm in
school. Sometimes I'm in England. Sometimes I'm in Britain.
Sometimes I'm a girl. Sometimes I'm a boy. Sometimes.

I want to be in extreme situations. I want to be in the condemned cell or
I want to be in the gas chamber. Beetle just off mother. I can't control
thoughts or think. Can't have no control over thoughts. Thinking.
Everyone seems to be trapped in the wrong bodies, in the wrong place,
in the wrong person. The wrong house. Trapped in the wrong house. I've
taken my pictures down off my wall.

I think at night in the dark, looking out the window at all the houses that
someone's going to turn it off. Turn it off or on. It's not real. I think I'm

in someone's argument. I cannot believe I exist. I cannot believe that it's all happening. I think that it's going to be switched off. How can you bear to have to live? I live in a TV set. I think of dying. How can we die, anyway?

Gary is very frustrated with pretty much everything and everyone, and his speech is an existential depiction of how he feels about what he sees around him and what he experiences inside his head. You need to think really carefully, from line to line, about the intentions behind each line, and precisely where each thought comes from. You need to work out which lines might be quotations of things you've heard other people say, and which aspects of the speech are conclusions you've drawn for yourself.

Gargantua

Carl Grose

This mad-cap caper is loosely based on a massive sixteenth-century book, which is also called Gargantua. This version is set in a small town in the present day, where Mr and Mrs Mungus have given birth to a giant baby whom they've named Hugh. To save the town from certain disaster, the Prime Minister sets his cabinet on red alert emergency over-drive. In this final scene, his adviser, Wellard, is trying to get the Prime Minister to remember the security code to open a huge safe-house door before the nuclear missiles hit.

Wellard   (*at top speed*) You give the go-ahead for a nuclear strike. We arrive here, the door seals shut behind us. You're about to punch in the entry code when – who's cooking onions? You collapse clean away. Prime Minister? Prime Minister! You wake up. You've lost your memory! Forgotten the entry code along with the past seven days! We re-play the whole event. The birth of Gargantua. The secret cloning plan. Agents are deployed. The giant baby is brought to Professor Swan. The people revolt. He escapes! Raahh! We attack! Booshh! We kill his parents. (Sorry!) He goes on the rampage! Bang! Crash! Impossible to stop! Stop! Prime Minister has no other choice! (Stop me!) We flee down here, to the safe-house! Please somebody! (I can't stop!) You go to punch in the entry code! Hmm! Onions? Bam! Prime Minister? You come around! Lost your memory! No entry code! Re-play the past seven days! Again! And again! And again! And—

(*beat*)

Prime Minister, the missiles launch in 30 seconds. Does any of this ring any bells?

This is a picture of a professional in panic. You need a lot of energy to perform it. You need to investigate what each point of punctuation might require, for example, 'who's cooking onions?' is a repeated joke throughout the play, and in this speech it is an aside which needs to be slipped in almost without you noticing it yourself. It is zany and absurd but for you, every intention must be absolutely rooted in truth; this is an emergency, a matter of life and death, and it will only be exhilarating for us if we can see and hear in you a genuine sense of panic.

Generation Next

Meera Syal

This play is set in three time zones: 1979, 2005 and the future. The location is always the same community centre in Southall, in which a Punjabi wedding is about to take place. This speech comes at the beginning of the play, in which Nina is about to marry Rikki during the early summer of 1979, and she is deliberating on the pros and cons of getting married at the age of eighteen.

Nina I mean course you think about it, hena? I mean, you're brought up that way, innit? What with singing lovers leaping into the bushes in the Bollywood movies and your aunties yapping in your ear as soon as you can roll a round chapatti, it's not like you can say No or anything. I mean you can say No if you don't like the fella, I mean if he's like too short or too greasy or a bud-bud just off the boat, I mean, have I got British Passport tattooed on me arse or what? Don't take me for no fool, innit!

Or, save me bhagwan, you might end up with a mummy's boy who's gonna throw you to your mother in law like a masala lamb chop to a starving jealous tiger, as soon as the wedding gold's packed away. I mean some of my mates, right, day after the wedding off come the coconuts and you're suddenly cleaning the toilet and trimming grandad's nose hair and sod off leaping into bushes cos you're probably doing the bleeding gardening as well.

So you think about it and you watch your parents worry themselves into wrinkles and grey hair saving for the big day cos of course, the bloke don't pay for nothing cos everyone's just so grateful some bugger's gonna take you off their hands and at least you ain't one of the saddos who end up at thirty still being touted round the temples and the matchmakers while everyone whispers, 'well if she's not married yet, there must be something wrong with her . . . see what happens to these career women? Too much thinking makes your ovaries dry up, no man wants to plant his son in a desert.' I wish I'd finished me college course though.

I could have said No. But our parents, look what they've given up, for us. They want to see us settled so they know the long journey was worth it. It's about family, not just me. I know I'm lucky really, getting Rikki.

Nina has an accent that is first-born London Indian: a mixture of street-wise London and glottal and expletive Punjabi. The important thing when performing this speech is to convey the life-loving character of Nina. She is street-smart rather than book-smart and cuts to the heart of the matter with very little hesitation or subtlety.

Gizmo

Alan Ayckbourn

The central character in this action-packed comedy is Ben. He is paralysed due to the psychological trauma he suffered at witnessing a shooting while he was working in a bar. He has had a 'gizmo', a microchip, fitted into his brain that is controlled by a wristwatch. Whoever wears the wristwatch determines Ben's actions. This is the story of what happened in the bar; Ben is in hospital telling his story to a nurse called Ted.

Ben   I was working in this bar.

There was this – young couple. Very flash, you know. Lots of jewellery. Good clothes.

It was early on. They were the only ones in there. Both sitting at the bar. He was showing off a bit. Obviously just met her. Wanting to make an impression. Lot of drinks. Champagne cocktails, vodka stingers. She could hardly stay on her stool.

They're sitting there laughing and suddenly this feller's in the doorway. I didn't even see him come in. I'm down the other end of the bar, you see, restocking the ginger ale. And he stands there this bloke and he calls out, 'Johnny' or 'Gianni' – maybe Gianni – anyway, this other bloke goes as white as a sheet. And the one in the doorway says it again, 'Hey, Gianni. Welcome home, Gianni.' And then he brings out this gun from under his coat and he shoots him, calmly as that. In his chest.

Right in the chest. And this bloke's coughing and there's blood everywhere and the girl's screaming and holding on to him. I don't know why she didn't get out of the way, I don't know why she had to hold on to him—? And this bloke starts shooting again – naturally he hits her as well, though I don't think he meant to particularly – though maybe he did – and all of a sudden they're both of them lying there. And he's dead and she's – she's making this terrible sort of whining. Like a dog – like when my dog broke its leg . . . And I know she's dying as well.

This bloke with the gun, he sort of looks down at them. And he smiles. It was the most frightening smile I've ever seen in my life. And then he turns and he looks straight at me. And he's still smiling. And he says,

'Okay, barman', he says, 'drinks on the house, eh?' And he starts walking towards me and I know then he's going to kill me, too. I know he is. Because I'd seen it all happen, you see. Like a rabbit.

Then someone came in from the street. They'd heard the shots and the screaming.

He dived round the counter and got out through the back.

Lucky escape.

All that blood. I've never seen so much blood.

He could've killed me.

As you work through this speech, you'll notice that it is constructed of long and short sentences. What is the effect of a short sentence after several long wordy phrases? You are describing a scene and what happened in it. How will you bring to life the voice of the hit man? In the early part of the speech you are using words sparingly to paint the picture in the listener's imagination – why do you think you choose to highlight certain details as you set up the context in which you're going to explain the key dramatic episode that led to your paralysis?

The Grandfathers

Rory Mullarkey

National Service ended half a century ago in the UK, but elsewhere in the world teenagers are still regularly conscripted into the armed forces. Following eight boys from training camp to the battlefields of an unknown war, this play presents in nine scenes, the extreme training regime a young conscript has to undergo before facing the frontline. Here, one of the conscripts, Dim, can't sleep, and talks partly to himself and partly to the other young soldiers who are slumbering in his dormitory.

Dim   Nights I wake up I think I'm covered in it. Mine, or someone else's, I can't be sure.

Slight pause.

Because that's what they say, isn't it, that when you're wounded that deep, when it really hits you bad that it doesn't actually feel of anything really, that you just feel I dunno kind of light and wet, obviously, from all the blood. There are others things that people can do, to make you feel the pain much more.

Slight pause.

Do you think about being captured? I do. Sarge says everything you can imagine has already been done, he says try and imagine something and it's happened, and that there are people whose job it is to imagine the worst thing and then to do it and these people have way worse imaginations than any of us. A wire round the testicles, a loop which lops them off, being nailed to things, having my eyes popped like balloons and then the dogs lick them out, my testicles in my mouth and all my skin going down my gullet that's what I imagine so that means it been done and that there's people to imagine worse. Sometimes I think it's better not to think. But they've done it, in the past, when it was just land that they wanted, just land that we wanted, but now the people that fight us and we fight have different ideas to us and we can't take their ideas off them like we took their land, we can cut off someone's nose but we can't drill into their head and cut out their ideas, so that just makes me wonder if it will ever ever end.

Slight pause.

I saw a video where they cut off a journalist's head. It wasn't as bad as I thought it would be. It was cleaner.

Slight pause.

And that'd be an alright way to go, maybe, well at least that'd be an end to it, at least that moment would be the worst moment of all, but I do worry more about other people, and what they'd say when they heard, how they'd feel, and whether that would be the worst moment for them too. My mum, you know, my mum particularly, because I love all my family of course I do, but I like really really like my mum. Coz just my dad, he. And my granddad. But my mum.

Slight pause.

And I know we've got parade in the morning, but still, these things. They're always there.

Pause.

Are you asleep? Is everyone asleep?

Dim has a thought-stream that at first may seem freewheeling but is in fact carefully sequenced and structured. You should think carefully about where to breathe in this speech, as that will enable you to produce the long unbroken phrases in a way that makes them sound as though they are coming out of your head in a continuous flow or rush of thought. You need to find Dim's state of mind: it is somewhere between controlled panic and time-suspended insomnia.

You should take care not to consciously 'play the fear or sadness' in the speech, but keep everything at the front of your head, so that what pours out are thoughts rather than feelings. Dim isn't called Dim because he's a bit stupid – it is because the lights in his head have been dimmed; he has become anaesthetized to the trauma and pain that soldiers experience. You should think about this when playing this speech; keep it factual rather than emotional. When you read the whole play, you'll realize that all the soldiers are given made-up names that make them sound vaguely Russian (which happens to be where the playwright researched some of the play), but his reason for keeping the names fairly non-specific, in terms of their context and location, is to make you imagine that this could be any conscript in any army, forced into national service at any time or place in the world.

The Guffin

Howard Brenton

This is a science fiction mystery story about a group of kids who attend a drama class each week. One of them, Jay, is in considerable distress because she is being intimidated by a couple of boys who keep verbally taunting her. This speech is performed by the character Sat, while he is developing an improvised speech as part of the drama class. The alarming irony about the speech is that it seems to accurately describe what is actually happening to Jay in real life. At the end of the speech there is a mention of the strange object, The Guffin, which, if touched, can change your life.

Sat   There's this kid. Everyone hates her. And she's annoying, like *very* annoying, always butting in. And she says really stupid things, and you try to be nice to her because she's, you know, her hairs all over, and there's something about her that really gives you brain damage, and you try to be nice to her but she screams in your face. So she is not a very popular bunny. But something's driving her mad, you see, inside her. Because she sees things differently. She sees colours that aren't there, aren't there for us, but are there for her. And if you could see a new colour, that others can't, how could you describe it? You say 'green' and green is green, but she'd have to say 'blug' or 'doob' or 'selt'. And when people look at her, they know that she's not seeing the world like we do. And it makes her feel so bad inside she could die. And because of what she is, she's a trouble magnet. And trouble she gets.

A beat. They are mesmerized.

She's going home one day. And she's seeing the world as all . . . 'blug' and 'doob' and 'selt'. She doesn't realise where she's going. She ends up down the dip. There are these two thugs. Skeggy and Dump. There are those brick flats, boarded up. By the railway. She runs down there. There's a door, the bottom rotted. She ducks down and gets under and in. It's dim. Outside, she can hear Skaggy and Dump shouting out for her: 'Slag! Come here! Slag! Ho! Come here ho! Slag!' Door. She pushes it. Dark room. Wet floor. She can just see a colour. One of hers. She tries to be still. Not breathe. Not think. Then . . . something moves. Across the floor? Rat? Rat? But it shines. No, it sort of glints. For a moment. It rolls beside her. She . . . reaches touch and touches it. It's hard. It's stone, it's

not stone, it's metal, it's not metal. She lifts it up and looks at it. And it
... it's alive and it ...

A silence. Again he has mesmerized them.

*This is a highly expressive speech, larger than life, which lends itself well
to vivid physical visual gestures of description, especially in the second
half. You really need to get under the lines and empower them with
action – galvanize it – let the words run like electricity through your
whole body. Strike a balance between a demonstration of a 'typical'
drama-class type improvisation and something that contains real truth,
which suggests the awful possibility that Sat might be talking about Jay
and that the things he's saying may be true, so the speech doesn't become
overly melodramatic.*

*Note that the speech contains 'made-up' words. Enjoy them. These are
used throughout the play, and are part of the surreal style of the world of
The Guffin.*

He's Talking

Nicholas Wright

Set in the mid-1960s this play is about a group of students who are politically active in South Africa. It is set in a sitting room in London after one of the students has had a lucky escape from being interviewed by the South African police. The play presents the same scene five times, and each time a little more information is revealed and questions about collaborating with a corrupt regime emerge.

Miles Well naturally I knew the *suitcase* was there. Luke had asked me to look after it for him. He said it was full of banned books . . . Karl Marx, Lenin, Gramophone-something . . .?

. . . and he wanted it out of the way in case his flat got raided. I said no problem. The truth is I was flattered to be asked. He'd never involved me in that side of his life, 'the struggle', as he called it. He probably thought I wasn't clever enough. We'd been best friends at school from Standard Two right up to Matric and on the rugby-pitch, which is where things counted at our school, we were pretty damn even, but he was always the brainy one.

So it's a Saturday afternoon, beautiful day, rock-climbing cancelled and I'm sitting listening to the cricket when Luke comes in through the patio door. He said the cops had let him go, but he still looked jumpy. He said, I've come to collect that suitcase. I said, 'Relax. Help yourself to a beer, you know where the fridge is.' I went down to the garage . . .

He pauses, upset.

I suddenly didn't trust him. First time ever. I knew that if I opened it, and it wasn't just books inside, it would destroy our friendship. But I couldn't stop myself. I forced the lock, and there were four fat putty-coloured sticks, wires, a couple of alarm-clocks and some other shit. I looked around and he was standing behind me. His face was white. I asked him, 'Did anyone follow you here?' He said, 'Don't worry, I did every zig-zag in the book, I've shaken them off. Now give me that, I've got to dispose of it.' I said, 'You do that. Take it out into the veld, set the timer to zero, stand close and blow yourself to hell. Now fuck off forever.' I never saw him again, so sadly that's how things stand between us.

He blows his nose.

Sorry about the emotion.

You are describing the events of that afternoon to a small group of students who you know well. It is an intimate speech that is about the moment in your life when you were heartbroken to discover that your friend was not telling you the truth, and what's more, he was involved in terrorist activity. To prepare the speech, you should go through it line by line, working out precisely what your attitude towards Luke was at each stage of the discovery about the suitcase and its contents. As you perform the speech, you have to re-live the sequence of events that afternoon moment by moment. To be believable and engaging, the speech needs to have precise moments of recollection associated with each beat of the story you are telling.

In South Africa, a veld is an open grassy landscape, like a large field.

The Heights

Lisa McGee

This play is about a girl called Lillie who makes up stories. She lives on a council estate called The Heights but can't leave her bedroom due to a rare allergy to daylight. She shares her creepy strange stories with a girl called Dara who steals into Lillie's flat on a dare. This is the first story that we hear in the play, and it is told to Dara and her friend Jacob.

Lillie   Once there was a nice woman.

The nice woman had lots of nice things but she wasn't happy.

Because it didn't matter how many nice things she had. She was still all alone.

What she really wanted was a baby.

So the nice woman hoped and wished and prayed:

'Please God. Please give me a baby. I'll love it, I'll look after it. I promise. Please God please.'

One day there was a knock at her door. She opened it and screamed with delight – a cradle sat on her step. She looked inside and there she was – her very own beautiful baby girl.

However she wasn't like other babies, this little girl was different, she was special.

This little girl was made entirely from glass. She had little glass hands and little glass fingers, little glass feet and little glass toes, a little glass mouth and two little glass eyes . . . even the hair on her head was glass. The nice woman didn't mind at all – she looked at her and said:

'You're the most beautiful thing I've ever seen. You're perfect.'

But she knew she had to be careful. She was so frightened her little glass girl might break that she made her lie still in a room full of feathers –

'It's safe in here. Nothing can hurt you in here.'

The nice woman sat beside her and read her stories but she never touched her.

'I might damage you, without meaning to, I never want to damage you.'

One night the little glass girl had a terrible dream.

It was a strange dream too, for although she'd never seen the ocean she dreamt she was drowning in it. She screamed and cried – she was so scared that the nice woman put her arms around her without thinking –

'There, there, ssh now, ssh.'

She comforted her until the little glass girl wasn't frightened anymore. They lay back together on the fluffy white feathers. A while later sunlight poured into the room. The nice woman opens her eyes. She must have fallen asleep. She's warm and wet. She looks down at her body – and for a moment she's confused. The fluffy white feathers have all turned red. They stick to her skin. Horrified she realises they're soaked in blood – her own blood – her arms and legs are decorated with hundreds of tiny cuts, her body is covered in the smallest shreds of glass. The little glass girl is gone. The nice woman starts to cry . . .

'All I did was fall asleep.'

Poor, poor nice woman – she held her little glass girl too tightly –

Now she's all alone again.

This speech is full of vivid visual descriptions and also the voice of the nice lady, which you have to make distinct from your own voice so that the audience knows when they are listening to the voice of the nice lady, rather than that of Lillie.

Heritage

Dafydd James

This play takes place on May Day. A group of odd-ball children have been specially chosen to close the day's festivities by singing the village anthem, and they are sent to a paddock outside the hall to rehearse. As they gather, all is clearly not well; the paddock is surrounded by a dangerous electric fence, Tubbsy is hiding a cat in his bag, Deirdre-May is grieving her Nanna, and Mark has turned up dressed as a stegosaurus. They soon begin to realize that they have been chosen for a much darker purpose. The play explores nationalism and the difficulties encountered when preserving a cultural heritage.

Lisa (*in hushed tones*) Now, stop it, Douglas! I must insist you stop it! You're over-reacting. Deidre-May's Nanna was bonkers. That's why she killed herself. She was doolally! End of story. Doo-la-lly. Just like her granddaughter – she talks to the dead!

And I must insist you stop it with these weird conspiracy theories. You've gone nuts over a tiny bit of patriotism . . . You think way too much. We can't all be as clever as you, Douglas. And actually, sometimes it's nice not to have to think. I mean: I for one was quite pleased not to have to make a wardrobe decision today. Because – often – I find it impossible deciding what to wear. Yes! I do! I find myself staring into the wardrobe. For hours! I can be there for hours! My mother thinks I'm lazy and that I take ages to get out of bed, but I've been standing there since six deciding between a tie-front and a denim. We have way too much choice! It's terrifying. I panic when I have to make any decision. Sometimes I panic so much I throw up. Isn't it lovely, just for once, Douglas . . . Isn't it lovely, just to be told what to do?

(*becoming manic*) Everything's fine! Everything's fine! Come on everyone. Chop, chop! Let's rehearse. Tubbsy, you really ought to be thinking about getting into your costume. Let's remind ourselves of who we are! I'm going to warm up now, and I really think it would be a good idea if other people joined in with me because if they don't I'm going to get very, very angry!

Lisa lives her life on a high frequency, she has a lot of energy and is a natural performer. Throughout the play you regularly correct people who call you Lisa – you want your name to be Liza, with a 'z', like Liza Minnelli. You want to be adored and you want to be a successful singer, and you're determined to succeed against the odds, and most crucially, by conforming to what you think the adults in the community expect of you.

Hood

Katherine Chandler

A riff on the legend of Robin Hood, this play charts the adventures of a broken family on an estate in which Robyn tries to keep her brothers and sisters in check while her mam has run off with a 'bacon-licking vegetarian' and her dad refuses to get out of his armchair. It is a play about socialism, kindness and poverty. It is a poetic, atmospheric play that employs language and images in an expressionistic way. In this speech, Robyn's brother, John, is talking about his prediction of his own future to his friend Nas.

John I got dreams. But I think you and me both know that there ain't much point in me having dreams Nas. I didn't have the start you got, so it ain't looking too good for me, I reckon.

Pause.

I'd like to be in politics Nas. Cos I reckon I'm good with people and what I've got is a good heart. I give a shit. So maybe that don't make me cut out for politics as it is now but what I also got on account of my Dad, is a revolutionary way of thinking, so maybe succeeding as a politician who gives a shit would be my personal revolution.
I'd like to be a politician who makes people change the way they thinks about themselves and the world. There's a line in a song my Dad used to play before. The line says 'Kindness knows no shame' and I reckons that if that was a mantra for people, I reckon that would change a lot of things.
It's under rated is Kindness. That's what I'd like to . . . I dunno . . .

Pause.

In ten years I'll be in some mental ward in some hospital.
That's if we still got hospitals Nas. I'll be there on account of my habitual use of marijuana. I'll have

developed some borderline psychotic state of
craziness. I'll be wrapping myself in silver foil and
avoiding people with hats. And the thing is, I'm not
dreading it. There's a part of me that is looking
forward to the complete and utter state of not
having a rational or sane thought again. Because even
though I'll be worrying about hats and silver foil I
won't have to think any more about the real stuff.

Pause.

The voices'll piss me off though, with me being a fan
of peace.

Pause.

We haven't got any money.
Hood is worried they are going to take us away.
Split us up.
Starting to look bad.
Starting to look really bad.

*John has smoked a lot of marijuana and the long-term effects of this
show in the temperature of his personality. Look up the song he
mentions and listen to the whole track. When you read the complete
play, carry out research on Che Guevara and the other political
characters mentioned.*

*There are two lines in the second half of the speech that the playwright
intends to be funny, to lighten the mood for a moment – can you work out
which ones they are? Why are they funny?*

*As you learn the speech and work on it, decide to what extent the
thoughts John is having are occurring inside his own head and how
much he actually wants to tell his friend, Nas – in other words, how
much of this speech is spoken thought and how much of it is information
that is intended to be actively communicated?*

*Have a look at the longest sentence in this speech, the one about John's
personal revolution. You need a big breath before starting that long
line, and you'll find that the line really captures what this speech is
about. Try hitting the 'lu' syllable in the word 'revolutions' the two
times that you have to say it, and give those two points the most*

significance – see if that helps you to shape the way you say that long and important line.

This next speech is spoken by John's friend Nas who is one of the family living in poverty. This speech comes about halfway through the play when Nas realizes that she could, somehow, achieve a different life for herself.

Nas   One day I'll be sat behind a big desk in a big office –
I'm seeing dark brown wood, is that oak or some shit –
it doesn't matter – because one day I'll be sat behind
my big brown desk and a shaft of sunlight will shine in
through my window and hit the bit of my desk that
I've been staring at blankly for the last fifteen minutes
but I won't even have realised that's what I've been
doing until this sunlight comes and hits me and that
sunlight reminds me of the time when I wanted to be
an artist. And I follow the gaze of the light. And I
follow it through the window and I look out of the
window, for the first time, not for the actual first
time but for the first time, properly and I see the
trees that are outside my window and I notice how
the sun hits the leaves and the light dances off them.
And I see sky and it's endless, the peace and space of
the sky, its depth and it's colours all of them hypnotic
and vivid, and the sun seems – what is it – and the sky
it seems – it seems eternal – and alive – and I am
mesmerised. And I am an artist – and I pick up a pencil
and I have a notebook on my desk and I start, I put
the pencil on the paper and I look at it, the blank
page and the nib of the pencil breaks, I put the pencil
down just at the moment that the sun disappears
behind a cloud.
I go to my window but the sun has gone and the
tree doesn't look the same.

Who do you think you're speaking to in this speech? Why are you speaking? Is it by thinking and the act of speaking that ideas form in your head? One of the fun challenges you'll find in this speech is making choices about which words to give weight, which words to 'hit'. It is a poetic speech and it is a combination of colloquial language and language that is more heightened and pointed. The trick is to find a way to deliver it so that the whole thing feels coherently part of one style, and you create a wholly rounded, convincing character.

Horizon

Matt Hartley

This play is about two sisters and their little brother. One sister works in a shop in Horizon's View and the other has just finished her exams and is hoping to go to university, but her family can't afford to support her to study further.

Sally   I'm not stopping, what's the point?! There's none. Should just not bother with anything. School, anything. Why care? Nobody cares back. Look at Holly, look at her, look what's she doing. She's the brightest here by a mile, she worked every hour, every single hour and look at her. Here. Trapped. Look at her and tell me what's the point in going to school tomorrow. Tell me?? Study hard, work my socks off, want to go places, places that just won't happen. So then what am I going to do? Work in Topshop all my life? Do you not get it Becky, do you not see it? If Holly ends up working there, if Holly does that, somebody as bright and as clever as her, what's going to happen to you? You so can't compete with her. You need her, you like need me to leave, you need us to go to uni to fill jobs up the food chain, to be like that cos if we don't what will happen to you? No job, it ripples down, look how your Dad lives, look how they treat him, take his job away give him nothing in return, make him feel guilty, cut his benefits, blame him for not having a job that doesn't exist, blame him for making you hungry and live on hand me downs, 'cos that's what will happen and I want to see you work. I want to see you happy in that shop, buying those things you always wanted but it's not gonna happen, it will happen to people like her, like Kelly, always splashing her Dad's cash, they're fine, go about spending money in shops that don't ever pay tax, places that just take and never give back, that mean that my chances get ripped in two because greedy people won't help me and you out, like there's no point and I say we might as well just start smashing places up, smashing them up. Topshop, Vodafone, all of them because we're doomed, there's nothing here for us, no future no nothing, just might as well fight it, rip up Starbucks, rip it all up, here, there, everywhere, because, they don't care about us, about our futures, they don't, otherwise they'd say it's not fair, you deserve better futures, it should be easy for you to go to uni, it should be easy for you to want to dream big. But they don't. And if this is my future then I'm not going to go there lying down. No way. I am going to fight, I am going to shout and I want to do it loudly and I want to do it now and I want to know who of you are with me? Want to know who wants to smash this stupid skyline? Who wants to tear it down? Who wants to do that? Who wants to burn this place to the ground? Who wants to do that? Who? Who? Who wants to join me?

Sally stares at them all.

Start work on this speech by dividing it up into units. Give each one a name; this will help you to have a very clear target and intention as you talk through your trajectory of thoughts in each section.

Hospital Food

Eugene O'Hare

This play is set in a teenage cancer hospital ward. All the characters are at various stages of treatment for different types of cancer. There is a special room in which they go to talk, where adults aren't allowed. One of the patients, Gus, decides he wants to escape rather than spend the remainder of his life in the ward. Josh agrees, reluctantly, to help him.

Josh   You know my Dad only learnt how to use the internet because I was diagnosed. He was prehistoric before that. But once he typed in Google, well – he was gone – tearing through cyber-space like a thing possessed. He musta typed in the word cancer a million times. That and big tits. He's definitely typed in big tits. When he does his two daily visits to me I wonder if one visit's for me and the other one's for him to get a perve at Nurse Barbara's double G's.

But mainly he went all Google crazy because he refused – refused to believe – that a hospital was the only place I could be cured, ye know? That there was something out there – some miracle – somewhere – out there. Maybe it was hiding in a Brazilian monastery or the Chinese had it – yeah, what was it? – Chinese pearl barley – he was buying that up in bulk. Selenium tablets, powdered grass. I think he even mentioned a coffee enema at one point – I nearly decked him. And apricots. Christ. I were shitting apricots for days before he finally gave it a rest. Then came the conspiracy theories – how all the big pharmas were suppressing a cure. Well that went on for a couple a months. Eventually he calmed down abit though. Learned to . . . breathe abit, ye know? And let them get on with it. Let me get on with it.

I'm saying it cos . . . ye know . . .?

They do go abit mental too . . . dads, mums. Sometimes at the start they're calm. Doesn't phase 'em almost. Cos he's not gonna die from it – my Josh? – fuck that Doctor Jones – out of the question – My Josh? – *Mine*?

Some go mental at the start and then calm towards the end – others? – well it's the other way round – or they go up and down or who knows what way – different people – different ways.

But they all go abit mental at some point. Hardly blame 'em. They feel it inside as well. Just not near as much as we do . . . but they *want* to – they *want* to feel it – what we feel. All of it. They want to feel the same and share it. All the pain, the shitting, the vomiting – the *fear*. And carry some of it, like, *with* you. Together. *With* you. Ye know?

If you take this speech on, you might want to read accounts that teenage cancer patients have posted online, especially on the website of the Teenage Cancer Trust, which helped with the research for this play. You'll discover that this speech is about an unexpected role-reversal in the son–father relationship; Josh finds he has more inner strength to cope with his illness than his father does, and realizes that unlike in his childhood, he is taking the lead and has acquired a confidence and a maturity that he may not have had when he was younger.

I'm Spilling My Heart Out Here

Stacey Gregg

*This play is about a girl called Wilson and her extraordinary group of
friends who experience some enormous life-changing events on an
ordinary day. This scene takes place about halfway through the play.
Sweep is a girl who is sitting with another girl, Jody, who is very drowsy
because she has been drinking alcohol. It is the middle of the night and
they're in a park.*

Sweep You're great. You get the most out of life and you don't even
abuse substances. Except the blood of Christ. Which as we all know is
just juice.

We're not that different.

I mean I just say stuff. To speak in your language Jodes, I bet even Jesus
just said stuff. Didn't he curse that fig tree? I mean its not even fig season
and the idiot curses it cos it doesn't have any figs surely that's just like
me? I'm always cursing things.

Believe it or not Jodes. I've only had a semi shag.

Don't tell anyone. Or I'll break your bloody legs. Don't know why
everyone has me down as some kind of – Cos I mean mum had me at
seventeen how stupid does everyone –? I am pretty upstanding, actually.
An upstanding human.

Me and Dom promised never to tell anyone. But we. Got to third base.

Then he started crying.

Just played the PS3 for a few hours.

I'm pretty *conservative.*

You're a good listener.

Wrote a poem last Tuesday.

*The extraordinary transitions in this speech should be great fun to play.
You are talking to Jody (referred to as Jodes) but she isn't really*

*listening. There is a sense that you are as much keeping yourself awake,
alert and entertained, as you are talking to Jody. Almost every line
introduces a new subject. Your challenge as an actor is to allow us to see
into your thought processes that take you from one thought to the next.
When you read the whole play you'll realize that this is a play about
growing up and the physical and chemical changes our bodies undergo
through the teenage years. It is in many respects a 'mucky' play; it
ventures into areas of teenage life that are not often discussed socially.
The key to playing this speech successfully is to learn to understand its
delightful combination of what is sad and what is painfully funny. The
playwright helps you out towards the end by starting a new line for each
change of mood. This gives you clues about where to change gear, where
to shift tack. The comedy comes from the unexpected switches in subject
matter.*

Illyria

Bryony Lavery

This is a play about the horrors of war for women. It is loosely a dark re-imagining of Shakespeare's Twelfth Night. The central character is a young journalist called Maria, who travels to Illyria, a beautiful country that has become famous for its war. Maria struggles to survive, both physically and mentally, and she eventually finds that reading is her only hope of survival.

Maria   You leave Illyria.
   File your story.
   The horror. The devastation.
   You blow up like a Michelin Woman.
   You have a baby.
   He's the most
   beautiful
   perfect
   baby in the world!
   Born into light warmth safety.
   Toast.
   Hot chocolate.
   He's a month old.
   It's January.
   As Madame put on her new
   sensible shoes
   You put on yours.
   You're on a walk.
   You walking, Christmas coat,
   pushing him, Spanking new pram,
   courtesy Grandma.
   You leave the dog-walkers behind.
   The joggers.

   You're in a wood.
   The sweet smell of rotting leaves.

   Then
   through the wood
   This Man
   His shoulders up

something . . . off about him
No shirt black pullover
he's not wearing a coat
walked past us
too close

                   not looking

never looks up . . .
in all your years of foreign reporting . . .
feeling the pop of a bullet beside your ear
here . . .
lying under a tree trunk in snow there . . .
looking up at the iron belly of a
gunship there . . .

nothing
compares to the terror you feel
thinking
someone is going to hurt your baby . . .
and

you look at him!

he knows you will kill

and he goes
You feel uncomfortable even
mentioning them in the same breath . . .

war
you
but until that wet day in the woods
you had not even begun
to understand the pain of war . . .

*Maria is describing the after-effects of the war when her life has
'returned to normal'.*

She is experiencing post-traumatic stress.

*What senses do you experience in the first part of the speech? What
contrasts do you notice? What do you think the effect of the very short
lines is for you the character, and also for the audience? Why are you
feeling compelled to tell the audience this story?*

In the Sweat

Naomi Wallace and Bruce McLeod

This play is set in a disused synagogue in East London. Scudder, a homeless boy, is living there and one day in desperation takes a security guard hostage and interrogates him with his friends, Nazreen and Fitch. The play explores themes of race, sexuality and poverty.

Nazreen Seven years ago. Yes. Like. Seven hundred. My sister, Mahfuza, and I, we went out to use the phone. To call for flowers. It was my mother's birthday and her favourites were – they were – yes. Mimosa. Small yellow flowers, thin stalks. Mimosa. They smell like dust. Almost sweet. I waited on the corner to make sure my mother did not see us making the call as she walked home from work. Mahfuza was older than me but smaller and had to stand on her toes to put the coins in and dial the number. And then suddenly they were there, three of them, tall, fast boys, who moved quick, quick. Like white flames they sprung up from the stone of the pavement.

One of them had a can and he circled the phone booth, wetting it like a dog. Another wedged something against the door so my sister could not get out. The third boy, I remember he was laughing but his laugh was strange, almost like crying. He lay broken pieces of wood against the door of the booth and lit the match. And suddenly it seemed the glass of the phone booth started to burn. My sister still had the receiver to her ear, but she was no longer speaking. Her mouth was open. So open. But no sound. And I had started to run towards her. But by then the flames were high and someone grabbed me and held me back. And Mahfuza's mouth was still open behind the flames, as though she were going to eat them. As though she could swallow them whole. And there was smoke, lots of it, and after some moments I could only see the top of Mahfuza's head in the booth, her black hair blacker than the smoke.

The neighbours got her out. In time. What does that mean? In time? In time for what? For months and months after I came home from school I sat with Mahfuza by the window. I wondered if she was looking out for the three young men. Afraid they might come back. But the expression on her face was not one of fear. It was not one of anything. And no matter how many times we bathed her, for years afterwards, her hair still smelled of smoke. It wouldn't wash out. There's nothing wrong with her body but she doesn't walk. There's nothing wrong with her mouth but she doesn't speak. I look at her and I think: 'She is my England.' No, I say. But the hands in her lap, they are cold. 'She is my England.' I say no. Not for me. For Mahfuza. Perhaps. Yes, for Mahfuza, that silence. Sometimes that's how it happens. But not for me. No, not that for me. This is it. Here. Right here, isn't it? Under our feet?

You are recounting, moment by moment, a terrifying incident. Notice how short each sentence is, that is because by saying each line, you are re-experiencing the sensation of the trauma. As you speak, be particularly aware of the effect of the consonants in the language; you'll be able to use them to create a vivid picture of what happened to you and your sister inside the phone box.

It Snows

Bryony Lavery, and Scott Graham & Steven Hoggett
for Frantic Assembly

This is a poetic physical show about how human interaction can suddenly change when the ordinary landscape is covered with a thick fall of snow.

Cameron   *is holding a complicated box.*
    It's finger-freezing-nose-running-bollocking-nut-nipping-cold
    It's not Christmas
    It's just after

He starts to open the box . . .

    Because my birthday is on Boxing Day every year
    Everybody
    Even my mogging *Mum* forgets my birthday
    So because she feels Mega-Guilty
    in the January Sales she always feels she's
    gotta buy me a *Top* gift . . .

Box is open.

    This year
    It's

He takes out . . .

    a digital camera

(*Very unimpressed.*) Right. That says 'I love you'

Drops the box on the ground. Points the camera at us.

    Stay still

He takes a photograph of us.

    Got it
    Round here though there's not much to make a great picture

He photographs the box on the ground.

    Stay still
    Got it

There's a weird girl living in the building opposite
She mostly looks back into her room. Which is weird. Right?
Sometimes she looks out of the window

Pause.

Come on . . .

Then she turns to look out.

Cameron *positions his camera.*

Stay still

He photographs her.

Got it
Otherwise
There's just streets
Streets
Streets
Buildings
Buildings
Buildings
School
Saturday job.
Streets
Streets
Streets
Oh
And yeah
Some Lads
That like to threaten you on a daily basis.

(*in* **Lads** *voices*) Oy!

Yo!
No!
Particularly if you're called Cameron Huntley . . .

(**Lads** *voices*)

Yo!
Cuntley!

(**Cameron**) *Huntley*

Cameron *Huntley.*

(**Lads**) What we said!

    Cuntley!
    Yo
    Yo
    Yo

They stick the camera somewhere inaccessible to him then turn and vanish.

Cameron *takes off his box hat and retrieves his inaccessible camera.*

    You get spots.
    Your body goes weird on you.
    Girls ignore you.
    Especially Caitlin Amoretti.

Precise choices of physical expression are crucial when preparing this speech. Cameron is an ordinary teenage boy. There is nothing eccentric or particularly emphatic about the way he presents himself or tells his stories. The style of the play is physical; it was created through workshops with actors and the company Frantic Assembly, working alongside playwright Bryony Lavery. Therefore, some elements of the story contained in this speech should be physicalized – it is up to you to create your own physical language to do this. It is not mime – in mime there are no words at all. In this stage-language, words and actions complement each other, creating the whole stage picture to tell the story. Have fun preparing this piece, but be ruthless when deciding which ideas to use, as it is easy to over-express and over-show each aspect of Cameron's tale; we must be able to see and hear clearly the heart of his predicament.

Just

Ali Smith

This is a fantastical surreal story about a girl called Victoria who is accused of a very English crime: stabbing someone in the back with a black umbrella. The other two main characters are Albert, a policeman, and a woman called Mrs Wright, who has a different set of values from Victoria. There is also an extraordinary chorus of townsfolk, who are obsessed with their pot plant.

Victoria Anyone looking at this case in the future won't hesitate to convict you *and* her for convicting me on a case more full of holes than a wormy old apple, more holes in it than there are in a teabag. You'll become famous – for a miscarriage of justice. Because I've been judged guilty in such a way that future law-makers will hold today up as the very evidence of the end of English law, believe me they will. Where's the jury that'd convict me? Where? Eh? Eh?

And I warn you. I will speak so well and so articulately and so straight to the heart and so truthfully to the world, that after I've sold my story to a million broadsheets and tabloids, and after I've attended the premiere of the multi-million-pound-grossing hard-hitting bio-movie of my life in which I'm played in my youth by Chloe Sevigny and in my more mature years by Meryl Streep, no-one in this ancient venerable United Kingdom, no-one in all the countries the world over, no-one who's naturally drawn to a good true story well-told, will be able to eat an apple again without thinking of you and me and what's happening right here, right now.

Technically, the thing you need to look out for in this speech is where to breathe, especially in the second paragraph, which contains an extremely long phrase. As you'll find when you read the play, this speech comes towards the end and there is something climactic and triumphant about it that requires a lot of passion as you defend yourself and protest your innocence to Albert and Mrs Wright.

A Letter to Lacey

Catherine Johnson

This play is about an abusive relationship that Kara decides to give up. She hears that her ex-boyfriend Reece has a new girlfriend called Lacey, and decides to write her a letter, warning her of the dangers of falling into an abusive relationship. The play goes backwards and forwards in time, over a period of about two and a half years. There are three Kara characters, each representing the various stages of the relationship. When Kara mentions Keeli towards the end of this speech, she is talking about her baby. This extract from the play is a section of the letter that Kara is writing to Lacey.

Kara   Yeh, Reece was soooo romantic. One minute I'm a prick-teaser if I don't do what he wants, the next I'm a slag, because I do what he wants. But he totally pushed the right buttons. I did feel he was looking out for me because, really, my Mum should have been the one teaching me about self-respect, but *she* didn't know the meaning of the word. I remember when my Dad had a go at her, she'd just sit there, taking it. Smiling, even, like she agreed with all the names he was calling her – and I'd be getting more and more wound up, wanting her to stick up for herself. And then I'd think, 'well, I can't blame him for getting mad at her – look at her, she's *pathetic*'. And when he finally left, I just ignored her for weeks.

Don't get me wrong – I love my Mum. But she's a pushover. She's all 'anything for a quiet life'. I was sneaking out and seeing Reece and she couldn't stop me.

I'm not going to be like that! Keeli is going to tell Mummy *everything* or she doesn't get to go out, simple as!

Although you're sitting at a laptop, typing an email, you have to re-live and imagine all the moments in your story as you describe them. It is important that you are really familiar with your whole story and all the events in this play to be able to do this speech well. You might find it helpful to consider which thoughts in the speech require only a little effort to find and which thoughts come flooding through your head in a way that is unstoppable.

Little Foot

Craig Higginson

*This play is set inside a network of underground caves in an
area known as the Cradle of Humankind in the outskirts of
Johannesburg. A group of school friends go exploring the
caves and come across the oldest human remains and a four million-
year-old ape-man known as Little Foot. The play
alternates between a realistic adventure story and an expression
of a nightmare. One of the group, known as Wizard, falls victim
to bullying by one of the stronger personalities called Moby.*

Moby Wizard. Always the coolest guy in class. The best looking. The
one the girls talk about. He forgets how well I know him. That I grew up
with him.

Do you even know why he's called Wizard? I do. I came up with the
name myself. I did it to help him out.

(*To* **Wizard**.) I was there when you pissed yourself during that tennis
lesson. You remember that?

The teacher was talking to us. We were huddled, in this
group – and Wizard, he was too shy to ask to go to the toilet.
I think we smelt the piss first. Or maybe we saw the dark puddle
spreading, around his feet. We all said – gross! And stood back,
to watch – the puddle growing towards us.

They used to call him 'Whizz' – which meant to piss – or 'the Whizz
Kid', because even then he was too clever for his own good. I can
still see him standing there. Leaking. And the tears running down his
face.

Wizard pissed away his whole childhood. He wet his bed until he was at
least fourteen. He once told me he was too afraid to go to sleep. In case
he pissed himself. So he'd lie in bed all through the night, waiting for the
first birds to sing. For a few years, he even started wearing nappies at
school. The teacher told us when he was off sick once that he had a
problem. A defective valve, or something. We weren't to tease him. But
that only encouraged them. Wizard was soon being laughed at by
everyone – to his face.

Even after the nappies went, he'd cry for days at a time. For no reason. Even when the others had forgotten, and moved on to someone else.

His mother took him to a psychologist. The psychologist blamed her. So she took him away again. We all know Wizard's Dad was killed when he was small. Murdered for his wallet. Shot in the back as he was running away –

Old Wizard – he was a pathetic sight. A blubbering joke. I was the only one who stood up for him.

And what thanks did I get? None at all.

So I started to call him Wizard. To turn his name into something positive. With a bit of magic in it. But Wizard originally comes from Whizz. Whizz the nappy-wearer. He was a sight for sore eyes. A Mommy's boy. A drip. A wet.

As you work through the speech, work out which lines are addressed to the group and which should be directed to Wizard himself. This will not only give you variety of focus, but will also vary the levels of tension throughout the storytelling.

Lunch in Venice

Nick Dear

In this play, a small group of students are seen eating pizza while sitting in a square near the Rialto Bridge in Venice. They talk among themselves about the works of art they have seen while on a school trip to Venice, and what they want to achieve in their lives. The twist comes late on in the play when we realize that all of the young characters are in fact dead, blown-up in a terrorist incident just before the play begins. There is, therefore, something slightly dreamlike about the play, something just out-of-focus, something other-worldly. Ben speaks in the glare of the midday sun, and he is dazzled by its light.

Ben (*to us*)   I'll tell you something in confidence. I was going to, you know, give it a try. With Bianca. Thought about it up the bell tower. Just let my hand fall on her arm . . . as we looked out over the lagoon . . . there was a moment . . . but my nerve failed. As usual. And the thing is, with women, there's a moment, and believe me I know what I'm talking about. There's a moment, and if it passes, and you haven't put your hand on her arm, you're dead. It's gone. You can be great mates. But you never get back to how it was before the moment when it might have become something else.

Oh yes, I'm a past master of the missed opportunity. I've got more female friends than I can count.

That pretty well sums up Venice for me. One more thing I should have done whilst I had the chance.

This is a speech in which you have to relive an episode from your recent past. As you move from sentence to sentence, think very specifically about each part of the episode in the bell tower that you are remembering. It may help to find photos of Venice, even specifically pictures that illustrate the vista across the lagoon that you're describing here, to help you imagine the circumstances you were in. You are directly addressing the audience – why are you confiding in them?

The Minotaur

Jan Maloney

*This verse play is based on the Greek myth, Theseus and the Minotaur.
Every year seven young men and seven young women are sent to the
island of Crete to be eaten by the Minotaur – a monster, half-man, half
bull. One of the seven, Theseus, with the help of Ariadne, manages to kill
the Minotaur and the Athenians escape. On fleeing to Crete, Theseus
then abandons Ariadne on the island of Naxos. This shocks Ariadne. This
is the moment when she wakes to find that Theseus and everyone else has
boarded the ship and sailed away, leaving her alone on the island.*

Ariadne   Aphrodite, goddess of love,
   You bitch!
   You filled me up with false hope
   The lust of love and the love of lust
   From the depths of my womb
   To the sparkling surface of my eyes
   You set me alight
   With a desire irresistible for my enemy
   Some bastard upstart Athenian prince
   Full of fire
   Warming every cell in my body
   Full of air
   Lightening my every thought
   Full of earth grounding me with desire to be grounded
   Full of water
   Crashing, flowing, filling up every space within me.
   All that for this,
   To be abandoned on a deserted shore
   For love I turned against my own father
   My own mother
   Daughter turned traitor
   Princess turned spy
   A curse on you, Theseus
   And on all your family worse.
   On all Athens I lay my curse,
   On all men. I warn women
   All women alive and yet to live

Do not give
Do not give freely of your love.
Beware!
In love you're in a minefield.
The man closest to your heart
May be a stranger.
Should the fancy take,
The moment turn,
Some vision of female beauty
Other than your own
Or political machination
Of which you are not aware
Maybe clicking in that power-crazed
Machine he calls his brain.
Beware!
His heart may be flowering
Yet his mind can deaden by decision
Love within the hour.
Do not believe the whispers of the night
Brought on by lust
Or sipping too much wine.
Do not trust for trusting him you make yourself the fool.
May my warning echo over the sea
And down the ages yet to come.
Give not your heart,
But hold onto your head.
Scheme, practice deception,
Do what you will, but banish
Honesty, purity, love.
Hide behind the mask and let not
Aphrodite have her wicked way.
For she will overturn reason, upset inner balance.
Banish her and all her wiles
Don't give into the pretence of men's smiles
But rule yourself,
Don't let some goddess hold sway
However powerful she may be.

You'll notice that the speech, like the whole play, is written in blank verse. The first quarter of the speech is a description of what your life

*has been like up to this point in the play. The immense turning point for
you is when you reach the realization and ask: 'All that for this?' After
that, you find yourself in an unstoppable downward spiral of anger; a
fury in which your personal experience is presented as a warning for all
womankind. It is a very impassioned speech, which borrows from the
Classical myth, but is written in language that feels fresh and common to
everyday speech. Play it with clarity and be fueled with unstoppable
force.*

The Miracle

Lin Coghlan

Ron and Zelda start helping people in their town after the flood. Ron's mysterious special power begins after the arrival of a statue in her bedroom. Ron helps a boy to read, a girl to eat and another boy to stop stealing. Eventually she gets in trouble with her headteacher who tells her to stop using her powers as they are causing concern among the townfolk.

Zelda   See, our street, our town, it's full of things that used to be different, things that have got stuck, things that are like shells of themselves. From the top of our street you can see the roof of the old Mill that's been empty for years and years . . .

And up the road there's the school with the bell where they had to close it down after the first world war when all the boys went to fight and only two came back . . .

There's the place that used to be a snooker hall, and then they made it a gym and then a kick boxing place and then a snooker hall again . . . there's the flats where the Irish lived, and then the Asians, and then the Turkish and then the Kurds . . . there's the house that used to be where old people went to die and then a residential care place for boys and then one of them clinics where you get needles stuck in you all over and then a sex shop . . .

And there's the people, my dad who wanted to be a policeman but wasn't tall enough so he went to work in Bentley's, behind the counter, and Ron's mum who was going to emigrate to Australia and work on a sheep farm but her sister got sick and she had to stay at home, and then it was too late for her to go because she had a husband and baby . . .

There were people all through those streets with problems, and it seemed to me only Ron here wanted to help. So anyhow, they made us promise, that it was finished, and we wouldn't do it no more.

Zelda is explaining why they have stopped helping people. The whole speech is always leading to the statement you make in the final line. The

*way you describe the changes in the town, the descriptions of things both
past and present, is justifying the underlying reason why you think it is
wrong that you have been stopped. You need to feed this intention into
the whole speech, although of course the listener won't realize the point
you are making until the end.*

Mobile Phone Show

Jim Cartwright

This play is a variety show of snatched stories, all of which involve a mobile phone in some way. In this speech, the young character, BB, is trying to locate a phone that he or she has just lost.

BB   I've lost me mobile!

To members of the Audience.

Anyone seen a phone?

You seen it! Phone? Phone? Arrrgh. You seen a phone? No idea where it is, looked everywhere! Me phone, seen it?

To someone in Audience.

Can I borrow yours mate, to call it?

He does.

It's Ringing. (*Listens.*)

To audience.

Sssssushhhh! (*to everyone*) Listen, can you all listen. There's a life at stake here!

Silence.

No. No. No. Nothing.

He gives phone back. Moves onto stage.

It's gone.

My whole life has gone. I've been murdered basically. My young life taken from me before my time!

Help me.

Think what's on there. Think. I don't want to!

It's my brain, everything I need to know comes from there. I've had a lobotomy basically, and my brains been left on the sideboard or under a

couch or a changing room bench, on a wall, at a bus stop or in a bin . . .
God forbid. It's my life. How can I go on!

How can anyone get to me! I've been off an hour they'll think I died. I
can't get hold of a soul. All me numbers everything. GET A NEW ONE
YOU MIGHT SAY! But it's all the stuff. Reaming reams of my life.
Scroll back the years and years of it. When you die they say your life
flashes before you, well mines on there!

All the best texts I got or I sent, works of art they was, some of them.

Some of those tender, tender ones I was keeping too.

Christ I've nothing now to show my kids!! When they come, if they
come, I'll never meet anybody now will I? Love life up the swanee!
Phoneless Romeo!

Without a phone, how do you date, tell me that? Go on tell me!

I could have passed that sim down through the centuries.

A heirloom.

I don't have to use me brain if it's all on there do I? I'll have to crank me
human one up now, where do you start?

It's the feel of it too, you get used to it, you know it and it knows you.
Like a gunslinger and his colt 45, Jimi Hendrix and his guitar, I could
work it in the pitch dark, I know it's every little phone foible, all its little
ways. (*He fills up.*)

Suddenly in shock.

Oh God, all the pictures, Irreplaceable, Oh God, the parties, the holidays,
the beaches – The one where I went like that . . .

He jumps in the air legs spread arms up.

. . . caught in mid air I was. No one will ever see the like of that again,
it's a moment in time. Oh God, my baby sister, our old dog that's gone,
concerts, me with the famous, arms round,_____(*Here can be inserted
celebrity names if desired.*) thumbs up. (*Puts his thumbs up like he's with
them again.*) And even one of me and the phone, I took in the mirror.

One offs, originals, the only copies, the . . . .

Suddenly in shock again.

OH GOD! and all the secrets, oh no, all the stuff, private. It can go
public now. I remember this happened to someone I heard of, they had to

move away, start a new life. They needed a complete new identity basically. Someone forwarded all the photos and all the texts and all the messages to everyone. Oh no! All the records of cheating and scamming and backstabbing and slagging all the naughty pictures of others I should never ever have took. That's me finished.

There's nothing for it, only one thing for it. I'm going to have to go on Facebook and tell all, get it out before it gets out.

Can't even get on facebook without it, have to use old Bessie the school computer.

Where do I start? There was that text . . . (*He cringes.*)

That photo . . .

That . . .

He suddenly pauses. He has heard something . . .

Wait a minute. Wait a cotton picking minute . . .

What's that I hear?

What's that?

The sound of angels . . .

That's it . . .

From a distance we hear a ring tone, it gets louder and louder, someone approaching with a phone.

BB *goes to take it, they lift it out of reach, then they run off laughing,* **BB** *gives chase.*

Come here.

BB *traps them.*

BB: Right!

Any Frapeing?

They shake their head.

Any breaking in?

Shake head.

Ok,

BB *kisses them on the forehead.*

Thanks. Thank you. I owe you everything.

Takes the phone.

Holds it on high.

Then checks it.

It's only been off an hour and there's 101 messages.

OMG. OMG.

Makes a call.

I'm back. I'm back, it's like a someone dying of thirst in the desert, suddenly drinking, drinking again . . .

Back . . . Back . . .

Turns away with the phone still talking ten to the dozen . . .

The crucial thing you need to do to make this speech work well is to keep it incredibly fresh, front-footed, and to strike up a personal electric engagement with your audience. You'll notice that it begins as a very naturalistic conversational piece and then slides into something more poetic. It's a good speech for letting traits of your own personality sing through. It will bring out the extrovert in you.

The Monstrum

Kellie Smith

This extraordinary tale takes place in one of the coldest towns on earth. Onley is a strange kid who takes body parts from the local hospital and builds a 'better' version of himself so that he won't be bullied at school but the creature he makes turns out to be a monster. In this speech, Beatrice is speaking directly to the audience and is standing by a model of the town and as she speaks she is shaking snow over it.

Beatrice   Imagine a place
　　The smallest village
　　In the highest mountains
　　This place is beautiful
　　　　if you saw it in a picture book
　　　　frosted little houses
　　　　shards of glass hanging from a wishing well
　　But this
　　This is the coldest place on earth
　　No, it's much much colder than that
　　It's so cold here that people's glasses freeze to their faces
　　Their ink turns to ice before it hits the page
　　Nothing will grow here
　　Even a turnip turns to glass
　　So the people eat horsemeat, and wolf meat and sometimes even
　　　　reindeer
　　You see
　　You have to be made of grit to live here
　　You have to be made of mountain rock
　　A little old lady will bludgeon a thief with a pickaxe here
　　People, here they can endure anything
　　Survive anything . . .
　　Well, almost anything.
　　Something has
　　Something has happened here
　　We don't speak of it
　　As you look at this scene
　　What do you see missing?

Men, women, children
But the youths . . .
My son . . .
My daughter . . .
Control yourself!
They're gone
It is a terrible secret
The thing that took them
Terrible, terrible
It's a disease!
Sssshhhh!
People here
In these parts
They call it . . .
The Monstrum

*The key to this speech is in the way you say the last word – everything
you say until then has been resisting saying the thing that everyone fears
most. Begin prep for this speech by creating a vivid image of what you
imagine the monstrum to look like, so that you know exactly what it is
that you are avoiding as you hook the audience into the atmospheric
location of the story.*

Moonfleece

Philip Ridley

This play is about the day when some young members of the British National Party turn up in a tower block flat where a young squatter called Link is living. Curtis, the son of Mr Avalon, leader of a right-wing political party currently campaigning in a by-election, has arranged to hold a séance in the family's old flat to communicate with his dead brother, who it seems was killed in a homophobic hate crime.

Curtis is 18 and a natural leader. Before this speech he has been describing the various members of his family in a photograph to Link.

Curtis Jesus Christ, haven't you heard *anything* I've said, you bloody stupid—? Listen! My Gran was one of the first people to move into this tower block. My Mum – she was born in this flat. She had her wedding reception in this flat. My Mum and Dad used to live in this flat. My first Dad. My *real* Dad. When Gran died the funeral procession left from this flat. The big bedroom down the hall? That's where Jason was born. Me too. The four of us lived here and we were bloody happy. Mum, Dad, Jason and me. Everyone respected Mum and Dad. They came to them for advice and stuff. If anyone had a complaint against a neighbour they didn't go to the council or anything. They went to Mum. They went to Dad. *They* sorted it out. Always. When Dad died – I tell you, the whole bloody block stood outside when the hearse drove past. And the flowers! The car park was covered. You could smell them right down to the supermarket. Local papers took photographs. We had drinks and sandwiches in here afterwards. Neighbours queued up for hours – hours! – to pay their respects. You see this armchair? Mum sat here and cried so much the cushions were wet for weeks. Months. Dad's death ripped her to bloody pieces. You ever seen that happen to someone you love? Eh? It's shit! I'd rather kill myself than see that again! My brother – Jason, my *real* brother – he had to look after me. He was seven years older. He washed my clothes and got me to school and . . . and cooked my dinner and . . . – Don't you *dare* refer to this flat as yours! Hear me? Don't *dare*! It'll *never* be yours. It'll never be anyone's except mine. Even when they dynamite the place – and it's nothing but rubble – the rubble that makes up this flat will have my name running through it!

In this next speech, Stacey tells of how Mr Avalon came to her aid the day she buried her dog.

Stacey   It was awful what happened to Jason, sweetheart. I never had the pleasure of meeting him but, from what I hear, he was a charming young man with everything before him. But sometimes, you know, things happen for a reason. We don't know the reason. Only him upstairs knows that. Right? It's like when my sausage dog died. I loved that sausage dog. Banger its name was. And one day I looked in its little basket and Banger was as stiff as a board. I cried and cried. Dad wasn't much help. He said we should use it as a draft excluder. I got no sympathy at all. Dad wouldn't let me even bury Banger in the back garden. So I wrapped Banger in some kitchen foil and took him over to the park. They had a flower garden there and I thought it would be nice to bury Banger amongst all those daffodils. So I dug a hole and put little Banger in. I was just covering Banger up with earth when I heard the Park Keeper yelling at me. Oh, the names he called me. The language. I ran and ran. He chased me. I ran all the way to the market. I was gasping. I went into this little Paki shop to get a can of something. I took something out the cooler and opened it and swigged a mouthful. Ooo, it was delicious. It really was. I put my hand in my pocket and – no money! Not a penny! I glanced up at the Paki and he was serving someone else. So I thought, I'll pop home and get the money and then I'll come back and pay the Paki later. I'd only taken one step out the bloody door when the Paki rushes over and grabs me arm and accuses me of stealing. Me! Well, I start screaming and shouting and giving the bloody Paki a piece of my mind. And that's when this man comes out the shop next door. A white man, thank God! The man pays the Paki the money I owe him and takes me into his own shop.

You are not directly associated with the family who lives in this flat and you feel to some extent an outsider in the situation. However, you have a very strong nerve and very little self-awareness. You're in company where you don't have to conceal your racism. When it emerges it should sound absolutely commonplace if it is going to be convincing.

More Light

Bryony Lavery

*This play takes place in the huge tomb of an ancient Emperor. The ladies
of the Emperor have been buried alive with him, so they can live out the
rest of their lives alongside his dead body. Becoming restless, they eat
the corpse of the Emperor to satisfy their hunger, and then they begin to
create art. In this scene, one of the women, Pure Joy, is being painted by
another lady called Love Mouth, and is trying to hold her poise while she
speaks to us.*

Pure Joy   Love Mouth draws all for a
    composite group portrait.
    None of us is moving.
    Trained only for politeness,
    respect towards servitude,
    we struggle like crawling toddlers
    towards the skills of creation.
    I am finding myself the stillest of us
    all for I am thinking.
    What art?
    Hundreds of years hence
    people will penetrate this tomb
    and they will see the painted sky
    studded with jewelled stars,
    the rivers of quicksilver,
    the mechanical archers,
    the gates,
    the bronze army,
    and say,
    'Look, it is the sky,
    the stars, the rivers, archers,
    the gates, and that must be
    the army!
    What Art!
    And look, in the middle of this section here,
    these skeletons, wrapped in fine clothes,
    these must be the women!
    What were they doing here?'

And one of them, keener-eyed than
the rest, may find, among the dust,
the shape of a bird
and he will touch it
and the old paper bird will
fall to dust,
and he will say,
'No, I was mistaken.
it is nothing,'
and will turn back to the beautiful
gold and silver gate.
So I keep still,
while my eyes and mind scamper and
scrape like a rat about this monument,
looking,
looking for the post and lintel
on which to rest the architecture
of my dis-ease,
for the arch to take the weight
of my fear,
for the rib vaults and flying buttresses
to hurl my hope stone-like
into the ether.

*Until they find themselves alone and able to do whatever they want, the
women have only ever known male artists, this is why they are tentatively
finding their way in their new-found endeavour to make art about what
they see around them. Notice the contrasting qualities the writer paints
between the fragility of the bird and the might of the army and the
machinery found inside the tomb.*

*The fun with this speech is to try to remain as still and posed as possible,
as you are in a graceful and beautiful position to have your full-length
portrait painted. You need to bring the story to life as energetically as
you can by using the full range of your voice; the humour will come from
the image of you attempting to stay still.*

Mugged

Andrew Payne

*Marky and Dig are two harmless lads who while away their time
chatting about life as they sit on a bench at the edge of the park near
their school. The park is reputedly full of 'muggers' and one day, in a
rare moment of courage, Marky finds himself confronting the muggers
when they steal his friend's phone and they stab him to death. This
speech comes at the end of the play and is spoken to the audience by his
best friend, Dig, who finds himself very confused by the way the local
community has responded to the death of his friend.*

Dig   I suppose God had to get in on the act sooner or later. Well, why
not, everybody else has. It's funny, Marky had this theory, right, that
if you really wanted something, you only got it when you stopped
wanting it. He got this theory because of his dad. Marky's dad was
supposed to come and take him out every Saturday but he was always
late or he'd never turn up, and Marky used to lie awake all Friday
night worrying about whether his dad was going to turn up or not, and
one night Marky thought 'Fuck it, I don't care anymore' and went to
sleep and the next day his dad turned up, bang on time, with a wicked
present. So that's where that theory came from, and I didn't really get
it, but I think I do now. Marky always wanted to do well at school –
without having to do any work, right – and suddenly he's this brilliant
student who was going to get 'A's in everything and go to University.
And Marky always wanted to be famous, and now he's famous. And he
wanted lots of friends – 'It's important to have a social
life, Dig' he used to say –

– and now he's got all these new friends, people who ignored him or
treated him like shit or didn't even know him in the first place, but it isn't
much good to him now, is it? So maybe that theory is bollocks.

Or maybe that's the whole point of it.

Anyway. All the things that have been said about Marky, the good things,
the bad things, they're all about someone else, this person called 'Mark
Bennett', they're not about *Marky*. Nobody seems to mind that, but I do,
cos I want to remember him properly.

What I want to remember is that Marky was my best friend. He was
funny. He invented weird drinks. He never did any work. He was
brilliant at nicking sweets. He once wore the same shirt for two weeks.
He had a theory about everything. He told the truth, not all the time, but
more than anybody else I know. And he was very brave. That's what
Marky was really like. And I'll never forget him.

*When you start this speech, you need to have established a very
comfortable and familiar connection with your audience before you even
draw your first breath. They need to feel they've known you all their
lives. You need to work through the whole play to learn and understand
what the references Dig makes about Marky refer to. This is a very
personal homage that a character makes to an audience that he assumes
is more understanding than the community in which he finds himself in
the play.*

Multiplex

Christopher William Hill

This play is a kaleidoscopic panorama of the stories of a bunch of kids working in a multiplex cinema. The pecking order is set and it leads to all sorts of confrontations between the various ushers and popcorn sellers. Frequently, characters step forward and tell the audience their story, and this is one such instance.

Spike   The thing about school, the teachers always seem to think if you're bright you *want* to learn. Like how wrong can you get? Can't wait to get out the fucking place. I can count to ten in three languages, so I reckon I'm educated enough. GCSE revision would be a fuck of a lot easier without the teachers there to distract me. Maths, English . . . piece of piss. So I spend half my time trying to find ways to get thrown out. So many fool proof ways. Art for instance, a gleaming example. You could shit on a piece of paper and call it post modernist sculpture. So I did. This does not impress old Mr Vincent. 'Call this art' he says, 'Yes sir' I said 'Very Tracey Emin, don't you think sir?' 'Tracey Emin my arse' he says 'It's a load of crap, that's what it is' and we all piss ourselves laughing, cause that's exactly what it is. 'It just won't wash' he says 'this is state education not the fucking Tate Modern'. He said buggering, not fucking, but I think fucking's what he meant. We call him 'the dick', old Mr Vincent, cause he's a bit of a dick. The clue's in the nickname. And the tosser says, 'Spike, you always have to have the last word'. So I say, 'yes'. So then I get suspended, which means I can have a lie in. Don't need to get up. Dad's pissed off to bugger knows where with Gran's care assistant, and mum's on the alcopops, so basically, my life's my own. And our deputy head, he's a prick, he keeps phoning up and saying 'you can come back to school as soon as you've learnt your lesson. Have you learnt your lesson yet?'. So of course, I say, 'Not yet sir. Might take another week or two'. And the twat can't think of nothing to say, so he says goodbye and hangs up, and I go back to watching porn on cable.

Beat.

Cushy number really, school.

Spike is a nice guy – doesn't cause any trouble, is uncomplicated. He is popular in an understated way. Play the truth of what he says and explains, and the humour will naturally present itself, don't force it – it won't be funny. You might want to try imitating Mr Vincent's voice/ accent; it is probably quite worldly-wise and retiring.

My Face

Nigel Williams

This play is about a group of friends who are all part of a group on a social media website. Typical anxieties that emerge online are explored, including racial stereotypes, assumptions and the tensions and arguments that follow.

Mark   You may wonder why I created an imaginary friend for Susie. Well – if you want to know I have been in love with Susie since we were in primary school. Ever since I saw her as the Virgin Mary in the school Nativity play. Being a Jew I have always had the hots for the Virgin Mary. I mean – what a woman! The blue hood! The donkey! The stable! The yellow haze round her head! And – have you noticed this – she never looks Jewish! The mother of the famous Jew in history and she looks like a fucking Nazi! Well – Susie – in my view – is a bit of Nazi. Which is exactly why I like her. And when she was playing the mother of Jesus at the age of nine I had real trouble keeping my dick in my trousers. I was a Roman soldier – in keeping with the unracial stereotypical casting of my primary school. But she never looked at me.

Mark is an extremely anxious and paranoid teenager. You must play him absolutely straight and invest in the trauma as much as possible. We find traumatic situations funny onstage, if they're couched in the right way. The less funny you find this, the better it'll be for us.

Don't shy away from the startling content in this speech; again, the humour and warmth of your character will come across the more confident and commonplace you treat the content of what he is telling us.

Nuts

Fausto Paravidino, translated by Zachary Kinney

A group of friends descend on Buddy's posh house and trash it. Years later, they are interrogated in a police station in an extreme way that is disproportionate to the crime they have actually committed. It is a play about collaboration and then a play about the extent to which we can reasonably punish people. The characters in this zany comedy are loosely based on those in the cartoon series Peanuts.

Snappy I'm hungry. I'm really hungry. Only I don't have any money, like, five – five bucks, you follow me? I go in, like, the first restaurant I find. It's expensive – all good stuff, but it's expensive. Check the menu, and I order what I can order with the money I have: one thing on the menu has, like, twelve ingredients, right, it costs less than everything but there's a lot of stuff in it. I look around: gigantic plates. Mine comes and it's a tiny starter. I eat it in two bites and instead of going away, my appetite got bigger. It was also really good. It was then that I lost it. I looked around and there was this guy eating something that would make your mouth water just talking about it. I grab the waiter and ask him for the same thing that he brought to the guy. Really nice, the waiter, says 'Yes sir.' After a little while he comes back with what I asked him for. And I lost control. I order drinks too and eat one hundred dollars worth of food. As the hunger begins to pass, anxiety starts to hit me, but I decide not to think about it until I have my coffee and after the coffee, I get a drink to boost my courage. At this point the waiter brings me a little plate with the bill folded in two and I don't open it – not even out of curiosity. The escape route is impossible because I'm a little weighted down and also a little tipsy. So then I start to think. I'm sitting there for a lifetime, no one comes to disturb me. But slowly the place begins to empty out and the waiters start to whisper, when one comes up to me to say . . . I beat him to it and I tell him that I would like to speak to the cook. The waiter asks me if by chance I wasn't satisfied and I say no, no, on the contrary. The cook comes and I look him right in the eyes. I give him a big smile, I stand up and say, 'This is the best meal I've ever eaten in my entire life. Unfortunately I don't have the money to pay for anything, but don't take it as a sign of disrespect, on the contrary. Because I don't have any money, I would have never have eaten so much if it hadn't been so good.' I was doing everything that I could do. I waited for a fist in the face or a reaction worthy of my speech.

He should have said, 'I work with my heart, as you yourself tasted with your palate, but after years of honored service, the sensation of working only because you are part of a machine like this is always stronger. Your speech has moved me. There are those such as yourself who help lift up those such as myself. Go, your faith has saved you.'

Try this speech in many different accents until you find one you think works well and in which you're happy performing. Then make a decision about what you want the audience to think of you – love you, hate you? Intrigued by you? It's a crazy play but we must believe that you exist and become captivated by your story.

Pass It On

Doug Lucie

This play is in four scenes, set in four significant moments of recent British political history. This is the third scene and is set during the early hours of the morning when New Labour has just won the General Election of 1997. Giles is drunk in a garden with his girlfriend, they are both members of the Young Conservatives.

Giles I suppose it'll be the same now. They'll all be screaming for equality while the country goes to the dogs. Why don't they ever understand? Some people are born to run things, others are born to make them run. And it always worked brilliantly. We ran half the world, for Christ's sake. But they threw it all away, just so that the bloody masses could have some of it and feel good about themselves. And, frankly, who ever cared how they felt? I tell you, the best thing we could have done would have been to make life as hard for them as we could, and if they didn't like it and started making trouble, great, send in the troops. Maggie showed the way with the bloody miners, but then those damn spineless nobodies got rid of her, and look where we ended up. With the Socialists in power. See, the Yanks have the right idea. As far as they're concerned, anything that happens in their backyard is their business. Look at South and Central America. Chile, Argentina, Nicaragua, El Salvador. The Yanks weren't about to let them go Communist, so what did they do? They helped the locals, the decent locals, get rid of the Socialist bastards and made sure they never had the chance to take power again. That's the way you do it. With a gun. If some jumped up little squirt wants to start a union and shout about workers' rights, cart him off somewhere, rip out his fingernails, stick a cattle prod up his arse and blow his brains out. Problem solved. (*Beat.*)

What this country could do with is a good dose of the truth. Fact: if you want the economy to work, leave it to us. Get government out of the picture. Fact: the Welfare State is an outmoded dinosaur that can't pay its way. Give it to the people who can make it work. Us. Fact: the country's being overrun by illegal immigrants and bogus asylum seekers. Strengthen the borders and set up bloody tough camps to house them in before we boot them back to where they came from.

Fact: there's no discipline in schools any more. Bring back discipline and corporal punishment. Not for us. We don't need it. I'm talking about the inner-city sink schools. The yobs. Give 'em a smack. Pour encourager les autres, as the old man always says. Fact: breakdown of discipline leads to crime. We need more powers for the police. We need tougher sentences, more prisons, life should mean life and bring back hanging.

Fact: there's too much regulation of business. Leave us to make things work the way we always have done. Fact: taxes are too high. Let people keep the money they earn and decide how they want to spend it. Chances are they won't want to throw it away on single mothers and benefits scroungers. (*Beat.*)

If I was to come out with that on Newsnight, I'd be strung up. You'd have Paxman and the Islington trendies baying for blood. The media have it all stitched up, you see. The grammar school boys have taken over the world, and they're almost all, to some degree, Socialist. Look what happened when Communism collapsed: all the Commies suddenly decided that liberal values were all right after all. And of course, they don't mean liberal the way we mean it, they mean quasi-Socialist social engineering. They still want to run the show, they just want to do it under a different coloured flag.

Carry out some research to find out what Young Conservatives were thinking in the mid- to late-1990s. John Major was the prime minister – were they surprised when he lost the election to Tony Blair and New Labour? Take the speech paragraph by paragraph and investigate the various political policies that you are clearly referring to in this speech. What do you imagine your family to be like? To what extent are your political views echoes of what your parents believe?

Prince of Denmark

Michael Lesslie

This play is set in Elsinore Castle about ten years before the familiar story of Hamlet by William Shakespeare. Laertes and his sister Ophelia are newly arrived in court and Laertes has got his eye on the throne of Denmark while his sister has got her eye on the young Danish prince, Hamlet.

Laertes Disguised as a player, he says? So, not content with debasing my sister, with ruining my family and stealing from me the only being precious enough to sustain a belief in the gods, this lecher lord is yet so embarrassed by his lust that he must carry out our humiliation in disguise! As a tawdry player! God's blood, his shame confirms his base intentions! This is no prince, this is a tyrant, one who views his subjects as fairground rides for venal entertainment! If he knew the nobility of soul my mother contained he would weep before he dared whisper to her youthful image, let alone board it, and yet this whore-maker will be king! Taken by the whole nation as the measure of a man! What then will happen to Denmark? I have seen him in court, glowering and mumbling to himself as though his troubles would defy the comprehension of mortal men, and we imitate our monarchs as pets their masters. Thus will Denmark be reduced to a nation of cowards, brooding solipsists so paralysed by soliloquy as to be blind to their social duty. And all for nothing. For convention. Why must this player be king? Why Hamlet and not another? My natural capacities are as strong as his. Stronger, my friends might say. Is it man's duty to accept the future handed down to him, or to arm himself against the will of fate and carve out his own fortune? What would happen, say, if Hamlet were removed from Denmark? If he were to fall from the cliffs this very night? Then the direct succession would be interrupted, and the King's brother would become heir. Claudius, my father's lord. And sure, I have seen that when the presumed line is thus disturbed, men's minds are opened to the true possibility of their limitless election. A meritocracy may be born. Then, who is to say that a peasant could not be king? Who is to say not Laertes? And would Denmark be better off? All for a push! I must act. Hamlet, make your peace. Your audience tonight will pay you handsomely for your player's costume. (*Glancing offstage.*) But hold, my tongue, for here comes a weapon in my plan.

*You're on the battlements, night has just fallen and there are
entertainments about to begin inside the castle. You have come out to
cool off, to contemplate recent events and to decide what to do next.
You're like a pressure cooker in need of release, and you might decide to
let out a burst of steam in the two words 'God's blood' – an exclamation
of utter disbelief at how Hamlet is behaving in the court. Once you've let
out this cry of rage, you'll find your mind is less tense and therefore able
to visit some ambitions which you may not have realized were in your
consciousness, until this moment.*

Pronoun

Evan Placey

Dean is a young person who was born a girl but now identifies as a boy. He has to deal with questions from his parents, his boyfriend Josh, and his friends. He also talks to a vision of 1950s icon, James Dean, who appears magically in his bedroom offering advice on how to dress and appear masculine.

This speech comes from the final section of the play when Dean is asked to make a speech to his school assembly and the Ofsted inspection team.

Dean   Good afternoon students, teachers, and visitors from Ofsted. Our school prides itself on tolerance. You can be who you want to be and we will tolerate you. It says so in a policy document in a drawer somewhere.
We learn in history about a black woman who decided one day to sit where she wanted to on a bus.
We learn about another woman who chained herself to parliament.
We learn about some angry drag queens in a bar who fought back one night.
We learn that to be tolerant of every person is what we should aspire to. A badge of honour we can wear. *I am a tolerant person.*

Fuck tolerance.

Those people – the black lady on the bus, the woman in chains, those men in heels. They weren't fighting for tolerance. To be tolerated.

Because tolerance is horseshit.

Tolerance is the emptiest word in the dictionary.

Tolerate is what you do when someone's playing their music loudly on the bus.

Tolerate is what you do when someone's texting next to you in the cinema.

I don't want to be tolerated.

I want to be admired.
I want to be envied.

I want to be . . . loved.

Love me.

And if that's too much to ask. Then hate me.
But don't tolerate me.
Because tolerance means sweet fuck all.

*The senior management of the school is not expecting you to say the
things you do in this speech. The turning point is obviously the line:
'Fuck tolerance'. You should relish the controlled, pressure-cooker-like
anger, which should surge beneath the surface of what you're saying.
You're not doing it merely to cause trouble, you're using language and
the moment to make a very big point; therefore, it is important when
performing this speech that we believe your thoughts come from a
deep-seated place of great tension. You must release your thoughts with
control as well as relief and passion, and take great care to present the
fullness of your story, desires and his beliefs.*

*Pronoun is a love story that follows Dean's life over the course of two
years of transition, and he renegotiates relationships with his parents, his
school, his boyfriend, his sister and his friends. In this speech he explains
to his boyfriend, Josh, the morning he realized that things were going to
be different.*

Dean   I woke up.

I woke up. I showered.

I woke up. I showered. And then the mirror was just there. Suddenly
there. Only it had always been there, but I'd, somehow, I'd managed to
never look. To never really look. Little tricks to avoid myself. But this
day, I was there reflecting back, naked. And it took a minute, prolly only
seconds, but felt like ages before I realised it was me. My body. And
without even thinking I crossed my arms, have you ever noticed – how I
always do that? For as long as I can remember I've always been doing
that. And I tried to make them go away. I tried to look away. Because I'd
never really looked. But I couldn't. This was me. And I hated it. Because
it wasn't me. Do you understand? My little cousin Adam, you met him at
my aunt's wedding, and she's always complaining because Adam won't
leave it alone – he's five and he won't stop playing with his willy.
Always investigating. I never did. Never investigated my own body.
Why? Why is that? I'm standing in front of this mirror, the steam fading
away, making the image clearer and clearer, this girl, this woman staring

back at me. And it was like everything clicked into place. People say your life flashes before your eyes before you die, well I wasn't dying but suddenly everything in my life was playing back. And in the mirror it all just suddenly made sense. Why I'd always felt a bit . . . wrong. And suddenly in my head, everything was . . . right. I'd never investigated, because I knew I wouldn't like what I found.

When you perform this speech, you need to choose something to represent the other character, Josh. This could be a chair or a post or something. It doesn't mean you need to direct the whole speech at that point, it just gives you a place where your story is landing. This is a speech that is as much for Josh as it is for the audience but it is important that we understand that it is an intimate story being told to someone you are very close to. The crucial moment in the speech is when you begin to relive the moment in the mirror: this was me and I hated it. You need to thoroughly investigate Dean's journey through the whole play to fully understand and be able to play this moment. There is an extraordinary silence after you ask Josh 'Do you understand?' The tragedy here is that he is desperately trying to understand, but he just can't get his head around it; you are only a little further towards understanding the predicament than he is. It is a speech about revelation and discovery, and should be played with a mixture of ordinary everyday life and a sense of immense wonder.

The Queen Must Die

David Farr

It is the night before the Queen's golden jubilee in 2002. Two gangs of young republican rebels plot to destroy a life-size papier mâché model of the Queen, which is due to appear in a carnival parade the following day. It is being stored in someone's living room, and the play turns into a farce as both groups attempt to steal into the room to destroy the statue.

Darren   Three months we've been thinking about this. Three months of precise planning. And now Les is busy. What would have happened to the French Revolution if the night before Danton had told Robespierre 'sorry, I'm busy'. There would have been no French Revolution, that's what.

France would be like England, ruled by a sovereign no one has voted for, responsible to no one, accountable to no one, supported by centuries of privilege and living in five massive palaces for no reason that anyone can possibly understand. You know what? Les did this on the anti-globalisation march as well. Remember what he said when he found out it was Macdonalds we were protesting against? 'I like the apple pies' That's not the point is it?

Try and get our useless generation to understand that politics requires commitment. It requires a level of sacrifice. We're talking about global slavery, extortion of the weak, we're talking basic human rights. So what if you can't get a frigging apple pie! Buy a Cox, and boil it! Try to understand we're not little consumers in our little consumer worlds, we can't just pick and choose beliefs like we're in a sweet shop. Well we'll show him. We'll do it on our own. Us three and Mary. That's all we need.

You're a very organized, slightly bossy, meticulous planner and schemer, working-class revolutionary, and you can't stand being let down. The key to doing this speech well is to be really swift with the digressions, breathe during a rare pause, and hammer home your serious points as if it's a life and death situation. The more seriously you take it, the funnier it'll be for us.

Ruckus in the Garden

David Farr

*When Riverdale Comprehensive and St Nectan's Grant Maintained find
themselves in the garden of Cecil Fortescue on a school trip
a ruckus is inevitable. It's customary that when these two schools meet,
violence ensues, and many of the pupils are relishing the opportunity of a
scrap. However, magic and mystery wait amongst the topiary in the form
of Cupid who brings about transformations and confusions, both
romantic and hilarious. With a nod towards* A Midsummer Night's
Dream, *this play is a fast-paced, entertaining look at the trials of being
fifteen.*

Cath   OK this is weird.
My clothes are different.
But he thought I was . . . He thought I was . . .
She . . . She's tall and . . .
She's a stunner.
I'm a dog.
But even the other boy blushed when he looked
at me.
No one has ever looked at me like that.
No one has ever touched me liked that.
Kissed me like that.
Who am I?
The lake! *She looks in the lake and uses it as a mirror.*
I'm her.
I'm so beautiful.
My legs go on forever.
My breasts defy all natural laws
My eyes are clear pools
My skin is polished marble
This is no ordinary garden.

Tamsen   What am I going to do?
I look like a member of the underclass.
Everyone is going to laugh at me.
Jocasta Mars Jones will piss herself.
Now she'll be the best looking girl in Year Ten.

I can't bear it!
I've got to take this off.
But then what – run through the garden in my
underwear?

A horrible thought. She checks under her top.

Aaggh! What has she done to me?
The most awful cheap bra the world has ever
known.
Oh some tropical bush come and swallow me
up! I just need to get out of here. Get home and
change.

She feels her clothes.

My purse. She's got my purse!
How can I get back with no money?
I'll kill her! I'll tear her limb from limb!
I have to find her.

*These two speeches are spoken by each girl in isolation. They are talking
to the audience. In the first, Cath, who is from the comprehensive school,
has discovered that her appearance has been magically transformed into
that of Tamsen, the posh girl.*

*In the second speech, the posh girl, Tamsen, has discovered that her
appearance has been transformed into that of Cath, the working class
girl. While riffing on the well-known lovers' scenes which take place in
the Athenian wood in* A Midsummer Night's Dream, *in which Puck gets
up to his mischief, these scenes also explore the theme of social class and
how the two sets of characters from the different schools identify
themselves as rivals due to their appearances.*

*When playing comedy like this, remember that the audience must not
know that you think the situation you are describing is in any way funny
– strangely, some of the best stage comedy occurs when we hear from a
character who is in deep trauma or humiliation within a set of
circumstances, and this is exactly what is happening, albeit with different
results, with these two girls.*

Same

Deborah Bruce

This play is set in an old people's home in the week that Josie dies. Her teenage grandchildren reminisce about their memories of her, and the residents of the home feel the effects of her death on their lives as her funeral takes place. The play asks whether the gulf between young and old is as wide as it feels, or whether we are fundamentally the same whatever age we are? The play requires young actors to play elders. In this speech, the character of Eddie is probably in his eighties – the magical quality of the storytelling requires Eddie to be played by as young an actor as possible.

Eddie   Because in it's hey day of course, you know, there were 25,000 dockers working on the Mersey. That's how it was. Up and down Great Homer Street, you'd get the smells, the fresh food being cooked up, from the markets. And we supported each other, the core of the society we were. None of your scroungers, and your wasters, sitting around on their backsides waiting to be given something for nothing. We earned a good wage, we knew our manners, always well turned out. I never heard my father swear, not once. Never owed a penny to anyone in his life. Not like these days. Not like the banks these days, messing it all up for everyone, throwing money around then wanting it back bigger. Langton, Brocklebank, Carrier, Canada, Huskisson, Sandon, Sandon Half Tide, Wellington. But in the 40s, 1947, I started, yes it was a going concern then, well over three quarters of us were dailies mind, not until the strike, and they guaranteed our working hours didn't they, it was a good wage. My father, honest to god, now, he never owed a penny to anyone in his life, not a penny. He was a gentleman. And his father, and *his* father. Settled in Scotland Road, he did, over from Ireland, 11 of them there were, 1845 it was. Worked on the docks since then we all have. Just 400 of them now. That's it. 400 left out of 25000. 150 of them in the terminal. There's not the loyalty now, not the solidarity. There was Seaforth, Gladstone, Hornby, Alexandra, Langton, Brocklebank, it was next along. But God's watching over me, 'Eddie', he said, 'Eddie, you listen to me. You have to let it go, nothing lasts forever, you're an old man now, and those days have gone.' I can see it, clear as you like, from the North side to the South, sun coming up first thing, 'alright Ed!' It went Huskisson, Sandon, Sandon Half Tide, Wellington, Bramley-Moore. 'Alright Ed!'

'Alright Robbie!' We looked out for each other, always watching my back, Robbie. Old Dock, Canning Half Tide, Albert. All the way down, mostly filled in now of course. 25,000 dockers we were, never took a day off work sick, never owed a penny to anyone in his life my father. Went to see Everton play every other weekend, like a religion it was, singing all the songs, talking about it all week, seeing us through.

> (*sings*) It's a grand old team to play for
> It's a grand old team to support
> And if you know your history
> It's enough to make your heart go ooo
> We don't care what the red side say
> What the heck do we care
> Cause we only know there's going to be a show
> When the Everton boys are there.

This is a memory recall speech and a celebration of a life. Eddie mourns the loss of a way of life for workers in the docks in Liverpool. You should take time to research the various places you talk about in the speech, look at photos taken at the time to imagine the area you're describing. You've had a very active life and are now confined to a chair in the sitting room of a care home. The speech ends with a song, which you should sing unaccompanied. It should have a fragile quality, but it also enables you to find an extraordinary inner strength, fueled by happy memories, as you remember singing songs like this with your friends.

Seventeen

Michael Gow

*Ella has been told by her parents that there is a history of madness on
her mother's side of the family that starts on their seventeenth birthday.
Shortly before she turns seventeen, Ella decides to run away with her
best friend to escape the family and the madness. Through a series of
mysterious and magical encounters, she discovers that madness is
relative. This play is a kaleidoscope of encounters and locations, and the
main character, Ella, is at the centre of the strange story at all times.
This speech is from the middle section of the play, where she is talking to
the audience. Her parents have just explained her family history to her.*

Ella I remember a wildlife documentary about the nervous system in
animals. In the wild, when they're being hunted and killed their bodies
are flooded with this drug that seems to numb them, block out what's
happening to them. That's all I could think of. I was like a zebra being
chased by a lion. I didn't feel anything. But this wasn't an animal party.
So we're sitting in our lounge room. No talking. I'm going to bed. I left
them sitting in the dark. Here I am in my room, where to now, what do I
do? On the internet, surfing for madness. Popular misconceptions,
history of mental illness, romanticism and madness, the effect of the
moon. There's even a test you can do, online, to see if you're depressed.
So many words, so many versions. What if they *are* watching where I go,
keeping track of what I'm looking at, entering data on this girl who
thinks she's crazy, then I'll never be able to prove I'm not, log off, shut
down. It's half past four in the morning, they've been talking for hours. I
just sit. Fall asleep, down into the dark.

*Ella is convinced throughout the play that she isn't mad. She presents
herself to her friends and the audience as a very level-headed young
woman. She works things out logically. That is what you are doing in this
speech – as well as being grounded in a very domestic reality, you need
to also find the magical elements and fill them with a sense of wonder.*

The Shoemaker's Incredible Wife

*Federico Garcia Lorca, translated
by Lucinda Coxon*

*This poetic story by the twentieth-century dramatist and poet Federico
Garcia Lorca is about an eighteen-year-old woman who marries an
older man who is a shoemaker. They live in a small house, which is also
his cobbler's shop in rural Spain. She has a totally different energy from
her husband, and a different set of expectations, which cause her to fly
into a raging temper virtually every day of their marriage. Eventually the
shoemaker abandons her and goes to live in a hotel; she turns the shop
into a bar. Although she remains faithful to him, the village treat her as a
strumpet. The shoemaker returns disguised as a showman running a
puppet-show, and realizes that she truly loves him, and they are
re-united.*

This speech is from the very first scene of the play.

Wife You shut your big mouth, you bitch on wheels! And let me tell
you: when I did it – when I married him, it was because I wanted to and
for no other reason! Oh, if you hadn't got inside your house I would have
knocked you down, you poison-tongued snake. Well make sure you hear
what I'm saying now, all of you hiding behind your windows: better to
be married to an old man than a blind man like you lot! And I don't want
any further discussion on the subject, not with you, not with anyone. Not
with anyone anyone anyone!

She slams the door shut.

I know better than to talk to people like that! Never even for a second.
No the blame's all mine – I should have stayed at home with . . . oh, I
can hardly believe it . . . with my husband. If someone had told me – me,
with this thick and glossy mane, with these bewitching eyes (come on
– credit where credit's due), with this figure and this exceptionally pretty
colouring . . . that I would go and marry a . . . I would have pulled out all
my hair.

*You'll notice that this speech falls into two halves. In the first half, you're
yelling at your neighbours who have been staring at you and whatever*

you've been doing as you try to live an everyday life. They've really got your blood up and you are letting rip. The second half is personal, private and contemplative, and we get to see what you're like behind closed doors. This speech clearly shows what you're like outside and inside the house. Enjoy finding the contrasts and being able to show two sides to this young woman's fiery and sensitive character.

A Shop Selling Speech

Sabrina Mahfouz

Present-day Cairo. Three armed robbers hold up a shop that sells speech tokens that can be used on street corners to enable residents to speak freely for the length of time that the token allows. This is a very stylish play about freedom of speech, which is tense in atmosphere and poetic in speech throughout. Ahmed is one of the workers in the shop, and here he remembers his brother.

Ahmed   My brother did what you do, many moons ago.
   He was my hero.
   He taught me everything I know, from coding to hacking to,
   well, things I won't share here.
   He went out on protests.
   Out onto the streets.
   Your precious streets.
   A real person, in action.
   Hands in the air, feet to the ground.
   Immoveable, incorruptible, a real person
   with a real heart and real hands
   and real flesh that bleeds when it is whipped
   and cut and carved and stamped and unstuck.
   He got arrested, we couldn't see him.
   Disappeared behind the sun,
   wara al shams, as we say.
   He was tortured in prison and
   he died. He was 21.
   So, Sahmia,
   I do realise the sacrifices that have been made.
   I just choose a different way than you
   to make sure they weren't in vain.

Notice how this speech has been laid out on the page. The structure of the verse will really help you to work out how to perform it. Look out for any words that may rhyme and decide whether you're going to acknowledge the rhyme sounds as you speak, or just allow the rhymes to take care of themselves as you deliver it. The Egyptian phrase 'wara al shams' means literally 'behind the sun', and it refers to the disappearance of political prisoners.

Shut Up

Andrew Payne

*This play is the story of a boy called Dexter who hasn't spoken for a year.
When he starts a new school, he gets into trouble for being violent, and
his parents begin to despair. The play is about coming to terms with
change, difference, and about finding the strength to have your own
voice.*

Tats   I told them what happened, Dexter.
I told them you didn't start it.

(*beat*)

But it was me against them. They
all lied. Richie and Bins. And
Anthony. I thought Anthony was
alright, but he does whatever
Richie says, he's such a wuss. They
are such wankers. And Chloe. She is
such a bitch. I hate them all.

(*beat*)

Richie was practically crying, and
you hardly touched him. What a
pussy. What a freak. I wish you had
hurt him. Really hurt him. If they
tried it again—

*Tats jumps to her feet, furiously kicks and punches the air
karate-style.*

I do kick-boxing. I'm a black belt.
Hi, Richie, how are you today? Bam!
In the balls, Richie! Bam! Bam! Hi
Chloe! Bam! Bam! In the throat,
Chloe! Bam! Chloe the Bitch! Bam!
Bam! Bam!

Tell them what really happened,
Dexter. Maybe they'd believe you.

Then they'd let you come back to
school, I know they would. It would
be so great if you came back to
school.

(*beat*)

Then we could hang out together. We wouldn't have to hang out with
    anybody else, we wouldn't need to, would we?
Would you like that, Dexter?

Beat. Then **Dexter** *nods.*

Say 'yes'.

No response from **Dexter**.

Go on.

(*beat*)

I won't tell anyone you talked.

(*beat*)

Say my name. Not Tats. Say
'Tatiana'. Go on. 'Tat-eee-arna'. Just once.

Dexter *doesn't respond.*

I'm going to ask you something, okay, and if you answer me, you
don't have to say anything else.

(*beat*)

For a year, okay? A whole year. We'll have an anniversary, okay? On
    the . . . whatever it is, I'll look it up when I get home, on this same
    day, every year, I ask you something and you answer me, and then
    you don't have to talk for another year. Okay?

No response from **Dexter**.

Okay? So here's this year's question. The first one ever. Okay?

(*beat*)

Okay?

(*beat*)

Do you like me, Dexter?

You're trying to get Dexter to speak. You're alone in a park and Dexter is sitting on a bench. Either use something like a chair to represent Dexter or ask a friend to sit on a bench and represent him, so you've someone to play off.

You need to learn some black belt kick-boxing moves. This speech is very energetic. When you realize that he isn't going to speak, even after all your vocal and physical exertion, the sense of disappointment should be immense.

The Snow Dragons

Lizzie Nunnery

*This play is based on historical events and is written in the style of a
folktale with music. It is set in 1940 and is about a group of Norwegian
children who form a resistance movement called The Snow Dragons
against the Nazi soldiers who are invading their town. Most of the play
takes place in the woods high up on a hill where they are keeping watch
on the town as it is occupied by the Germans. Here Christi explains to
the other members of the group what he encountered when in the town on
his latest mission.*

Christi   I saw my Granddad down there. I was so close I couldn't help
it – took the old turn down the old street . . . and I could see him sat up in
the front room like always. Except he was sitting in the dark. Sat up and
staring . . . and his face . . . His lip all swollen and his cheeks all
scratched. And he was so thin and white. And maybe I made a sound on
the gravel or something 'cause he turned and looked my way and I nearly
shouted. I nearly shouted out to him because he's got no one else. He's
got no one but me and he's in there in the dark on his own. But then I
realised . . . he wasn't looking at me. Just reflections on the glass . . .
Like I wasn't there at all.

*Christi can be played as either a boy or a girl. He is very agile and
climbs trees all the time, so he is the member of the group who is always
keeping an eye out for what is going on. Draw on personal experience in
this speech, to help you to imagine what the situation would be like if you
were faced with this extraordinary danger. The combination of acute fear
of the unknown forces of the enemy and warm familiarity with family is
potent. Technically, notice how many 's' sounds you need to use and
think carefully about how you can use the repetition of this sound to
create an atmosphere of fear and tension.*

*In the play, Snorri tells this story during a bombing raid to keep
everyone's hopes up. It is a story about good triumphing over evil, about
survival, about optimism.*

Snorri   There was . . . There was a . . . There was a little town on a
fjord. And one day shadows came swooping over. And the shadows
weren't monsters, they were machines. And inside the machines there
were men. But from the mountain tops . . . Odin saw all of this . . . And
he went leaping over the woods, thrusting the shadows away with a great
sweep of his sword, so the dark machines were scattered like . . . dust . . .
crashing against the mountainside. Then he pulled up a hollowed out tree
and used it as a horn to signal his brother Thor who was out on his boat.
And Thor paddled his oars and thrashed up a towering storm so the
waves washed over the town and put out the fires. Then he strode
through the waters, picking up the bad men between his fingers and
casting them out to sea like worms for the fishes.

Then Odin and Thor began to sing. They sang to the wolves using
strange wolf words, so everyone knew the fear was past. And Odin held
out his cloak and scooped up all the townspeople, riding away with them,
up past the woods and the mountains and the sky, up to a better place that
could never be bombed or broken but looked a lot like home. Like home
was before. With the little wooden houses dark red and yellow and green.
And the white washing flapping whenever the sun was out. And the
market stalls with all the same things in the same order and the people
having all the same conversations. And the fishing boats calling out to
each other in the early mornings. And salt pork ribs on Fridays. And trout
flapping and squirming on the harbour. And my Mum's at the back door
shouting for me to come in. It's the end of the day and there's no more
playing out. And my Grandad's in a grouch 'cause his team lost and I've
walked snow in the house again. But I make him a cup of tea and he
forgets all about it. And there's a crack above my bed where the water
gets through in the winter. And I watch it while my brothers snore at
night. And there's birds nesting up in the attic with all their soft scratchy
sounds. And Mad Finn'll be out wandering, singing made up songs
before it's light. And if it snows even the footsteps and the voices'll be
put to bed. Buried in the drift. And nothing ever changes. Not one thing.

*The consistent use of the word 'And' at the beginning of a line should
create a cumulative effect in the imagination of the listener, one of
happiness being invincible – you should be aware that this is the effect
you are creating as you tell the story: this is why you are telling the story.*

Soundclash

Lenny Henry

This hip-hop musical is about a small group of friends who have been challenged to put together a reggae sound system to perform at a 'Sound Clash', a recreation of a legendary music competition between DJs and MCs. None of them have the money or the equipment, but they do know a little kid whose dad used to be a DJ, who may have what it takes to enable them to triumph over the threat of DJ Emperor and the posh Claughton Kids from the school down the road.

Lil Kid   Walkin' to school from home in the morning
   My endz so real i can never be yawning
   Gotta stay sharp, round here's not boring
   You might get blazed your mom left in mourning
   Torn and forlorn wish you'd never been born
   Council estates not nice green lawns
   Guns and a knife are just part of life
   So please don't tell me to look on the bright side
   I just can't see one living round here
   Just tryin' not to get tump down here
   Ain't no coward just bein' realistic,
   'i ain't tryin' to end up as a statistic
   Statistic: sutten you don't ever wanna be
   mom's raised you alone and your dad's not free
   Statistic: when you've dropped out of school
   Try act hard but feel like a fool
   Truth be told – we ain't really that bad
   Take a proper look around – it's really quite sad
   We all act hard and then become scarred
   Left lyin' in a coffin or locked behind bars

DJ Emperor   Who's shoes are you steppin on?
   Gonna need a teflon-
   Vest to protect ya neck
   From our weapons son
   Fools never learn,
   I burn scalps like a perm
   My trainers cost more than a year

Of what your family earn
I cut you so wide, they'll need a rope
To stitch you closed
This is my hood here
And everybody knows
Makin' foes with me?
Prepare a date for your funeral
Shank ya man every other day
That's my usual past time
Was a warrior in my past life
Far's right now i got no cares regards life
So you better hope you got a crew to defend you
Cos if not, then right now, i'm gonna end you.

Lil Kid and DJ Emperor introduce themselves at the beginning of this play in the landscape of a street where a stabbing has taken place. Lil Kid is a seemingly vulnerable weedy kid, and Emperor is the alpha-male supremo from the 'other school'. They clash all the way through the play until a startling final scene in which Lil Kid exacts his revenge to the bullying with tragic consequence. Both speeches use a strong stylized rhythm. Enjoy finding your beat as you work out how to play these two speeches. They should be performed much larger than life, and with a lot of breath and style.

The Spider Men

Ursula Rani Sarma

This play is about various events triggered by sexual awakenings in a small group of older teenagers who live in a small town. The story centres around two teenage boys called Michael and David who stay out in the woods all night to escape the claustrophobic atmosphere at home with their respective parents. This speech is from the early part of the play and is spoken directly to the audience by David's sister, Sarah.

Sarah I got my nose pierced the day it happened. I'd wanted to have it done for ages but my Mum said my Dad would go insane, although to be honest I don't think he'd notice if I pierced both my eyebrows, my lip, my nose, my ears and got a tattoo that said slut across my forehead. Because he's not that kind of Dad. He's the kind of Dad that works all day and then comes home and sits in front of the telly and doesn't talk to anyone for the night kind of Dad. It's like my Mum threatens us with him just so we'll think he gives a shit but we know he doesn't. (*beat*) I read in a magazine about this girl who really wanted to get to know her parents, she turned fifteen and she wanted to form an 'adult relationship' with them but as far as I could see all that meant is that she wanted to talk about sex with them. I can't think of anything worse than having to talk about sex with my parents. It's disgusting. I mean when you talk about something, part of you is making little pictures in your head to go along with it even if you don't want it to. You know, like if I say to you, whatever you do . . . don't think of a pink elephant. (*beat*) What are you thinking of? (*beat*) See? So match that with talking about sex with your parents. (*Makes a face.*) It's just . . . disgusting.

My Mum comes in to my room that morning, I turn and look at her like, did you knock? I don't think so. She sits on the edge of my bed, without asking, and watches me do my hair so I say. 'What you want?' And she says, 'Sarah', in that fucking horrible way that makes me hate my name, 'Sarah are you smoking marijuana'. And the way she said it, 'm-a-r-i-j-u-a-n-a' and the stupid way she looks at me like I might actually confide in her . . . that's a joke . . . confide . . . in her? I tell her no and get out. She won't go so I say 'seriously get out, I mean it'. She says 'I'm worried about you, the school has sent a letter, there are kids smoking between classes'. I say get out. And she won't go so I scream 'Get Out!' I say 'you think I couldn't smoke fucking crack if I wanted to but I don't, I chose not to, I chose life alright, now get out! (*beat*) Now she thinks I smoke crack. (*beat*) Fuck her.

What clues can you find about Sarah's character in the speech? Make a list; this will help you to build up a bigger picture of her, her background, her family life. It's important to think carefully about breath while playing this speech. Work your way through it marking the places where you think you should take a breath and where it would be effective to continue through. You should also think about which key-word you should aim to 'hit' (or place emphasis on) within a long phrase. Also, ask yourself what the function of the 'beat' is? Is there a point at which this speech becomes amusing for the listener? Where and why does this happen?

Starstone

Christian Martin, translated by Penny Black

This is about a man who was abandoned during a war when he was a baby, rescued by a couple and brought up as the twin to their own daughter. When they're grown up, Starstone and Anna fall in love. He is conscripted to the army, which attacks the town where his adoptive family lives.

Thematically there are similarities with Brecht's epic plays The Caucasian Chalk Circle *and* Mother Courage.

Military Padre   so my brothers
the battle lies ahead
but do not do as others do
and say
I'll take the money
and serve the devil
because you
you are noble and brave warriors
serving the honour of god
you believe in righteousness
you fight for the holy fatherland
but
the enemy is real
and is entrenched
behind walls of stone
and its jeers are
weighted with hatred
it alone wants
to destroy us
and so spake the lord our god
'look
I will stretch out my hand
against the philistines
and smite them
and revenge myself upon them
and punish them cruelly
that they might know

that I am the Lord their God
and I will revenge myself
upon them'
but ye shall
behave and fight
as true christians
show mercy
spare the innocent
so now the time has come
unsheathe your swords
and fight
in the name of the lord our god
amen

*This is a highly poetic speech. It is not naturalistic at all. You should
approach it quite formally. You need to choose a word to 'hit' or aim for
in each one of these short lines. Is it the noun or the verb or perhaps
neither of them, and the stress lands on an auxiliary word? As long as
you make a clear and reasoned decision about which word in each short
phrase you think deserves most weight, the speech will make sense.*

Status Update

Tim Etchells

This play is a presentation by ten actors (named A – J) who stand on stage and talk to the audience. Each section of their speeches begins with the words 'We know . . .' The type of information and the way the speakers make propositions and assumptions is very varied throughout. The overall effect is a portrayal of collected knowledge of a group of young people.

B   We know that the behaviour of animals can be modified or conditioned using the deliberate and consistent application of particular systems of reward and punishment. Rats placed in closed box – sometimes called a Skinner Box or operant conditioning chamber – easily learn that the pressing of a particular lever is linked with the arrival of food, or with the cessation of an unpleasant electrical current. We know that there is little difference between the learning that takes place in humans and that in other animals. B.F. Skinner proposed that the way humans learn behaviour is much the same as the way rats learn to press a lever. Skinner believed that human free will was actually an illusion, maintaining instead that human action was best understood as *the result of the consequences* of that same action. If the consequences of an action were bad, there was a high chance that that particular action would not be repeated; however if the consequences were good, the actions that led to it would be reinforced and were therefore more likely to be repeated in future. Skinner called this the principle of reinforcement.

A way of approaching a speech like this is to make decisions and choices about the hierarchy of information that is given in the speech. Which sentence do you think is the most important, the most crucial? If you were only allowed to utter one sentence, which one would it be? Then build the way you do the rest of the speech around that pinnacle. You can also make choices about which sentence you find to be: 'the most cheering', 'the most amusing', 'the most reassuring', 'the most devastating' etc.

Stone Moon

Judith Johnson

This play is about a community in which women work in quarries and have arranged marriages in which they are not allowed to become pregnant for the first five years of the marriage. Kiri is sixteen. She has an affair with a man, becomes pregnant, and is thrown out of the society.

Kiri   The moon is big in the sky tonight, big and cruel and cold. Pulling the tides of the earth back and forth, controlling the waters of the world. They say us humans are mostly made of water. They say that the moon pulls on our bodies, pulls us like a swing, then lets us go: reeling, swinging, back and forwards like the tides. I want that from the moon. I want its power to pull me forward, drag me out of myself, send me reeling. Out of control. I want it from the moon because I can't do it for myself. Even standing here, just standing here outside, is too much. Even thinking these thoughts by myself outside while they sit inside and wait is too big a movement for me. People everywhere, celebrating this meeting of two families, this happy event, and all I can feel is frustration. Even the moon looks back at me with disapproval on its face.

You'll feel the sensation of great movement in the universe in this piece, back and forth, and a very certain sense of your own isolation and stillness in your personal situation: you're outside your house, while inside, your parents and Shem's parents are drinking tea and having a celebration. You feel very connected to the elements, the atmosphere, the universe – far more so than you feel connected to your family and the society of people you live in. The phrases 'too much' and 'too big' have weight that is heavier than you can bear.

Success

Nick Drake

Based on Hogarth's series of paintings The Rake's Progress, *this is a morality play with a contemporary setting. The story revolves around a young city boy, Tom Rakewell, who makes a fortune and loses it all. His journey around a dystopian city leads him to falling in love with a waitress, being led astray by the dangerous Nick Shadow, and being rescued by the mysterious bag-lady. It is a stylish, poetic play, which takes place in a series of slightly unreal locations.*

Tom Rakewell *is getting dressed in front of a mirror.*

None of it suits him, really.

He has a briefcase with him.

Tom Rakewell   I've never had a party. But Nick Shadow
    says it's the right time. He says it has
    to be the best party in history. He says
    it's my chance to get ahead. To
    capitalise on my success. It's cost a
    fortune. Literally. I've given it almost
    all I've got. But I'm keeping that a
    secret. Thank god for credit. To the max!
    Here's to success!

He kisses the case and puts it behind the mirror.

    All my friends have city pads and country
    estates, and stretches of coastline. They
    have forests, and hunting lodges, and
    helipads on castellated roofs. But the
    truth is I just don't get the countryside.
    I love the song of my mobile
    phone, not the song of the thrush. I like
    Ikea, not Antiques. I'm from the suburbs.
    Dirty word, I know. I hated the place.
    Careful lawns and careful hedges, careful
    cars and careful savings. My mates all
    ran away; they went backpacking for a

year and a day. Not me. I got a job. I
went to work. They sent me e-cards from
temples in jungles, and hidden beaches,
and the highest waterfalls. And they'd
say; *Cool! Awesome! Wow!* And I'd just
delete the lot. Because I'd found what
they were seeking: the lost treasure.

*To prepare for this speech, you should get to know the world of the whole
play and your character. You need to gather some research about city
gents like Tom Rakewell, and assemble a set of character qualities so
that you can build your own version of who your Tom is. How does he
speak? What accent? What has he changed about himself, voice and
appearance, since he moved to the city? Who is he talking to in this
speech? Is it the audience? If so, who does he think the audience are –
what impresses them? So much will be revealed about your character by
the way you say certain lines, as much as the lines themselves.*

Take Away

Jackie Kay

This is a magical fable play, in which the whole town is in the grip of onions. People of all ages are hooked on onions, and the onions are dominating their existence. A mysterious man called Darcus appears with a flute and promises the town council he will rid the town of their onion problem. The play is set in and around the town's take away shop. This scene takes place halfway through the play. The lonely boy, Kenneth, talks to the audience, explaining what has happened to him recently in his life.

Kenneth I used to like when I was a little fellow playing with an abacus and arranging the colours. And then I liked those puzzles where you had to arrange the numbers in squares. And then I liked those cube things where you had to get a whole side of yellow and a whole side of red. I was good at all that. And my mum used to buy me lots of those metal puzzles and I was good at those too. And then my mum died. She just died. And I'm not good at anything now.

I'm good at onions. That's what I'm good at.

(**Kenneth** *obsessively plays with the onions rearranging them into different configurations.*)

I liked that girl in the take-away tonight. She got me to say what I wanted, not like the guy. She had something nice about her. Not like him. He was a fool. But she was nice. If I see her on her own I'm going to ask her if she'll go out with me. My mum said if I had friends I would be happy and I said she was my friend and she said she wasn't enough and then she died and she definitely wasn't enough. Maybe that girl would like me. Maybe she'd like my onions.

I never had many special friends. Some people don't.

I was always a bit of a loner, a bit of a freak, a bit of an anorak. Just when I try and do something normal, I spoil it, at the last minute, and say something weird. I can't help myself. I know when I'm going to do it, like you know when you're going to fall and then you fall anyway. You can't stop yourself. It's something to do with gravity.

Kenneth is a young man who suffers from a kind of depression following the death of his mother, and seeks connection with people of his own age but finds that challenging and confusing. Kenneth is a very still character. He probably doesn't speak much to the other people who live in his town, but when alone on stage, he is quietly confident when confiding in the audience about his feelings and situation. When you read the whole play, you'll discover that onions feature in almost every scene, and each set of characters have their own particular relationship with them. For Kenneth, the onions have taken the place of an ordinary healthy social life. He is entranced by them. The hope for Kenneth is that he has recently met a girl of his age called Kimberley in the take away shop, and he has just about realized that she might be a helpful influence in his life.

Taking Breath

Sarah Daniels

While protesting to protect a tree from being cut down so that a road can be built, Elliot jumps out of the tree and knocks himself out. Standing like distraught statues at his bedside are his sister, Rachel, and his step-brother, Steve. Elliot suddenly sits up out of his coma and speaks the following speech to the audience while Rachel and Steve remain completely frozen, looking at the unconscious Elliot.

Elliot   Would you look at them? Look how upset they are. This is revenge I've only ever been able to fantasise about. They're sorry now. Yes! Even him. Look at him. He's always hated me and now he's paying for it. The times he's threatened to kill me. Ha, ha. He's my step brother. Thank God. If I'd had his genes in me, I'd have killed myself. And her, my big sister, Rachel. She's like just like a cat. You know how evil they are, swiping at a bird or a mouse, maiming it, then playing around with it for the sheer pleasure of being spiteful? Well, they most probably learnt how to do that from her. Let me give you a for instance. The first time I brought a girl to the house who, by the way, Rachel insisted on referring to as 'Elliot's babe'. Like if girls are sexist it doesn't count or what? Anyway, I was weary because she was being a bit too curly-lipped-okay-friendly. Then she produces it. When I was eight Mum used to be an agent for Kays Catalogue. I once drew over the underwear pages, crudely embellishing the photos of the models with the help of a felt tip pen by sketching in the rude bits that the underwear was covering. And, unknown to me, my sister, the sadistic pervert, had kept it for all those years waiting for the perfect moment to expose me if you'll pardon the expression. She didn't actually show it to the girl or anything but the threat was there all evening. I hope she remembers that now and every other humiliating little thing she's done and I hope she's so sorry she's thinking suicidally. At least she and me have the same Dad. Did have. He died of cancer when I was two. (*About Steve.*) But him. His Mum just got pissed off and went. And I know, I know kids aren't meant to be blamed for that but there's got to be exceptions to every rule and he's one of them. His Dad shacked up with Mum and then buggered off leaving him with her. She could hardly chuck him out. He's twenty now and the only job he could get was as a scab. The only thing he seems able to cook for himself is toast with brown sauce on.

He can't seem to get the hang of any of the basics in life, like white things should be washed separately in the machine. Mum still has to do his ironing. Where is she, though? She should be here, shouldn't she, at my bedside? Mum? Oh no. Now, I remember. She's away. I hope they haven't dragged her back. It's the first time she's been away without us. Maybe it's me. Maybe I've been away years. No, I can't have. Those two look exactly the same. This is now. I am Elliot. I am here. I am here, now. How did I get here? Where was I to get here now? Try to remember Elliot. (*He shuts his eyes.*)

At the beginning of the speech, you're referencing the two other characters standing by your bed, so you need to work out how you're going to present this – you might just explain the situation, or perhaps use two chairs to represent these people. You should also make a decision about whether or not you are going to perform this speech standing up or sitting down, or even lying on the floor as if in a bed, propped up on your elbows.

The Things She Sees

Ben Power after a novella by Charles Boyle

Dizzy is a fourteen-year-old girl who has a special power: she can draw the future. Her dad goes missing and she befriends Tad to help find him. They travel around London, talking to various characters who know her dad for various reasons, and they use her drawings as clues to help her find him. The play is narrated by an older version of Tad, and is set in various streets and cafés around West London. The play was developed with the aim of it being a very visual piece of storytelling; the stage directions that explain what the audience might be seeing during the storytelling have been left in to help you have an impression of what might be in view as you are telling this particular part of the story.

Sayyid I'm glad to see you Tadeusz.

Djanira and I thought it was time you learnt a little more about her father and grandfather. If you are to help us, it would be best if you were fully informed. Sit down here and I'll tell you a story. (**Tad** *sits.*)

Djanira's father is named Mohammed and it was he who came to England first. (**Young Mohammed** *appears.*) Mohammed was born among the Berber people, but had always hungered to be elsewhere. Because he wasn't a prophet like his father and his famous grandfather, the village believed that he must have offended the spirits. Aged fourteen he left the mountains and came down to the town of Meknes, where he became an electrician.

Four years later, he left Morocco completely. (**Young Mohammed** *meets another young man.*) My father met him two weeks after he arrived in London. It was 1973. Dad'd been here six months and showed Mohammed a little of London life. They drank beer, they watched football, they learnt English. And one day Mohamed met a Scottish woman in a bar and he married her. That was Djanira's mother. (*We see* **Young Mohammed** *meeting* **Young Kathy**.)

Then things got tricky. My father died and Mohammed took care of me and my mother. Then his own father, back in Morocco, became ill. He needed special treatment. So Mohammed arranged for his father and mother to come to London. They moved them into this tiny flat. (*We see younger versions of* **Dizzy's Grandparents** *arriving in London.*) Little

Djanira was only two years old. Mohammed's father was a devout Muslim – he disapproved of his son drinking alcohol, mixing so freely with English people, and he disapproved of his wife. The feeling was mutual and the tension grew. Eventually, Djanira's mother met another man in another bar and went back to Scotland. (**Young Kathy** *disappears from the group.*)

Life was easier then. But, as the years passed, Mohammed's father, Dawoud, became homesick. Although he'd been ill and would have died if he had not come to London, he blamed Mohammed for taking him away from the only world he knew, the Berber village. (*To* **Dizzy**.) But he never blames you. Her grandad loves Djanira very much. He's very proud of her. She has the gift.

This is a story-telling speech. You're a nineteen-year-old man who is a friend of Djanira's father. The two young children meet you in a council flat where Dizzy's grandfather is living. As you learn this speech, you need to work out which sections or lines are painting a picture of the past, and which thoughts are spoken directly to the two young listeners in the room, Tad and Dizzy.

Those Legs

Noel Clarke

This play is set in a city apartment and is about a young woman called Georgia who used to be a model until she was hit by a car and is no longer able to use her legs and now uses a wheelchair. She lives in the flat with three friends. In this speech, she confides to her friend, Leon, that she doesn't feel the same as she did before the accident.

Georgia He just wants a release. I want to be wanted. Haven't you ever wanted me? Don't you want me when you see me lying here? Like a guy wants a girl? Isn't there . . . that primal instinct in you? Something that just makes you want to take me . . . because that's what I used to get. I could walk into any room and men wanted me, I could feel their eyes, burning into me, their thoughts stripping me, and I didn't want or need any of their chauvinistic, sexist objectification. You know why? Because I felt good about myself. I felt like it was my choice. But I never knew how much I needed it until it wasn't there. We all need it a bit on some level, and now I'm here, paralysed, begging you to have me because I need to know that people, someone, still feels that . . . I need to feel something, because where I was is just a chair. People open doors for the chair, talk to the chair, smile at the chair – and me . . . I'm just . . . Invisible.

As you'll discover when reading the full play, you begin by talking about your boyfriend Aaron in this speech. The night before, he has slept with your friend, Lana, in the room next door, and hearing them together made you vomit and fall out of bed. You realize that your relationship with Aaron is over, and you tentatively ask Leon if he is interested in you.

Tomorrow I'll Be Happy

Jonathan Harvey

Darren talks to Scott as they sit outside eating crisps looking across at a splendid view of the sea. This play is about a homophobic hate crime in which Darren is violently stabbed to death by a small group of his school mates who fear what it is to be different. The play's scenes are organized in reverse order. The play therefore begins with the funeral, then the events surrounding the murder, and then we see Darren before his death, during happier days, before the hatred made itself a presence in his life.

Darren   I wish I was getting on a coach with you. Going somewhere. Anywhere.

Let's do it. Let's run away. I'm serious. You and me.

Somewhere we can lose ourselves. I've saved a grand and a half. I'll take care of you. We'll be all right. Get on a coach. See where it takes us. Find a little flat. Find some work. I'm serious. I want it to be night again. You don't care then. I can say whatever I like then and you agree. Or laugh.

They sit in silence for a while.

Yesterday the dishwashers packed in. All at the same time. Major drama. But instead of chucking money at it and getting 'em fixed they're making us wash everything by hand. The new routine. Have to go out and collect the dirty plates. Take them back to our station. Then wait our turn to use the platewash. It's this old thing with brushes sticking out the water. You rub the plate on it and. Well it ain't much fun for me. Coz I'm third station from the platewash. So by the time I get there the water's filthy. My manager she goes. 'Don't worry Darren. This time next year you could be first station from the platewash.' But I just know. That isn't going to happen. You don't know what's around the corner. You can be feeling lousy. Shit. But the next day everything's all right. So anytime I feel crap I just tell myself. Tomorrow. Tomorrow I'll be happy.

You are happy in this speech and unaware of the fate that awaits you, but the irony is that the audience is fully aware, as they have seen the rest of

your life played out in the preceding scenes. The play's scenes run
backwards, from the funeral to this final scene, which is a very early scene
in the relationship between you and Scott. Therefore, you must play it
without knowledge of what lies ahead, full of optimism and hope. You're a
very forward-looking character, who finds good in everything, and always
hopes that things will turn out well. You have fallen in love with Scott. It is
a very generous love but one that is never going to be reciprocated, as
Scott cannot allow himself to feel the same way about you.

Too Fast

Douglas Maxwell

This play takes place in the side-room of a church in a small town. A dozen young people aged thirteen to sixteen are waiting in a state of nervous tension because they are to sing a song at the end of a funeral of a girl from their school who was killed in a road traffic accident. Spoke's Brother has just been into the church to do a reading, he is about thirteen years old, the youngest of the characters in the room. He talks a lot, and doesn't seem to mind that the others give him very little respect or attention.

Spoke's Brother   Wait a minute. What the hell am I doing back in here? I was supposed to go and sit with my mum

and dad! Sake. Oh well. Would you all like to know how it went?

Would it be useful if I describe, in detail, my recent experiences?

To give you, you know, an idea of what awaits you on the other side?

(*Beat.*) He looks around, they are trying to ignore him, but he continues speaking as if they are all rapt.

Yeah it went okay actually. Nervous though see. (*His hands are shaking.*)

I was alright until I looked up. They're even standing outside, all the way up the gravel to the graveyard. And there's speakers out there so everyone can hear. But a stand must've broken or something because Mr Gibbons is up on a plastic chair, holding a speaker in both hands, like this. I thought, god, whatever I say next will vibrate in his arms. It'll go all the way back to the graves.

And when I looked back down at the reading I couldn't make out the words anymore. I could see them, but as like, marks on paper, not as real words with meanings. I heard someone say 'poor kid'. But I wasn't upset. Well, not until then. Cos then, after that, the meanings kind of came into focus. And now it did seem sad. Sad that all these words – every word from now on in – will vibrate nowhere near Ali. And I thought 'Poor Kid'.

But I just read it. Without thinking or feeling or meaning or anything. And got off. I concentrated on not tripping and

anyway, it went okay apart from, you know, coming back in here.

As Spoke's Brother speaks, the various characters in the room start to tune in to what he is saying; by the end of his speech they are all rapt. We don't know the character's name in the play, and this is intentional, as you are very much a satellite to the main group of friends and you feel like the outsider in many respects. You are the younger brother who never stops talking. You feel very much adrift in this company, the other characters, the people who are listening to you; they are only a couple of years older but it feels like a huge gap within your peer group. You feel like a young child trying to communicate with tall adults. The reason why you talk is that you can't bear silence. You talk as a way of trying to connect with the other people around you. Throughout the play what you say initially appears to be sprawling waffle, but eventually we realize that you have remarkably perceptive insight into the situation at the heart of the play. Although you articulate in a circuitous and splintered way, what you have to say in the end is illuminating for both the people in the room and the audience.

Totally Over You

Mark Ravenhill

Four girls dump their boyfriends so that they can date celebrities instead. Not to be outdone, the four boys form a boy band and say they've signed a record deal, so that they can make the girls jealous when they come running back to them. This comedy is about celebrity and love, and is based on a one act play by Molière called Les Précieuses Ridicules.

Letitia   I want to be my character again. Just a bit longer. It was so exciting. I mean she's a boring person but still . . . I made up a whole biography and everything. Like I lost myself. I never had that happen before. I mean I've been in plays and that. But I was always like 'Look at me'. Or sometimes 'I look terrible. Don't look at me'. And I'd always be looking over at my dad with the camcorder. But then, just now, I was gone. Like if I'd look in the mirror I wouldn't have recognised myself. Did you feel like that? When you were up there singing and you were pretending to be in that band? Wasn't pretending exciting?

Letitia is talking to Jake, and they're alone. This is towards the end of the play. It is the aftermath following all the pretence. You feel a huge sense of disappointment after what has happened, now that the fantasy is over. You begin to compare 'real life' with 'make-believe' and you find the reality hard going.

Travel Club and Boy Soldier

Wole Soyinka

While on a school trip in the South Sea islands, a group of wealthy European schoolchildren are taken hostage at an airport and have their passports taken from them. A boy soldier visits them in the room where they're being held hostage and asks them to collaborate with their captors. This speech is by one of the boys in the class who describes and defends his own cultural heritage, while trying to remain calm and level-headed in the circumstances.

Fabori   I don't need other people's lessons, Danny Boy. We had our own share of that business you know. The Biafran War, remember? My cousin was only a child then, no more than four. He told me of the day they came into the Midwest. They went from house to house, flushing out the Igbo. Marched them away. He was not Igbo, though it took a while for his guardian to persuade them that he was simply a ward of the family. His parents had died in a motor accident and these old family friends had adopted him. His guardian was determined that my cousin should be spared, even though he knew he was going to his own death. He forced my cousin to speak a few words in his own language – at four years, you understand? Still, he managed to convince them . . .

Later of course, the relations found their bodies in a mass grave. And even before the war itself began . . . in the northern parts, it was not good to be an Igbo. But I do agree with you – for once. There is no point fighting this.

There is no point jumping to conclusions. And you don't argue with a man with a gun, especially in a business you know nothing about. Why should I stick my head out of the window when there's a hailstorm pounding the roof? That is a very wise proverb from my part of the world.

My cousin's guardian stuck his head out. He was a doomed man. He did his duty by the child of an old friend. For whom am I supposed to be performing this duty? And what duty? I don't know what the hell is going on, only that we are trapped here and our gaolers have demanded something that is of no use whatsoever to me. Why should I make an issue of it?

*You are very confused by the situation you find yourself in, you don't
know what is going on in the room, or outside it, but you do have a clear
understanding of what happened in the Biafran War, and you're
assuming that the motives of your captors are similar to those of the
insurgents in that conflict. You're trying to use your knowledge of the
past to gain a grip on the uncertainty and trauma of the present.*

A Vampire Story

Moira Buffini

The play is about Ella and her claims to be a vampire, two centuries old. She lives with an older girl called Claire who might be her sister but might also be her mother. At school, she makes friends with a boy called Frank who has been home-schooled to the age of sixteen and finds it difficult to connect. The school is concerned about Ella's increasingly bizarre fantasy life. We never find out for sure whether Ella is a vampire or not. This speech is given at the end of the play by the teacher called Fillet to Ella and her class in a food technology lesson. Fillet is an eccentric food technology teacher. He or she has just learned of the extraordinary and mysterious death at the school of a colleague, Mint.

Fillet   In order to do my proper duty to you as a teacher of Food Technology I have been trying to teach you about every edible thing on this planet. We've gone into the Earth and returned bearing fruits. We've spent many weeks delving into the vegetable. And now we must encounter the beast. A new heading. Meat. This lesson may bring you learning that will affect the rest of your life. I want you young people to leave my class secure in the knowledge that if society broke down and all the supermarkets closed, you could walk into a field, butcher an animal and prepare enough food to feed a village for a week

I'm harking back to a purer time, when we didn't consume meat from factory abattoirs, vacuum sealed in plastic, I'm harking back to a time when we stroked and petted every beast we ate

If we killed it, we'd respect it.

I am going to teach you to respect the beast. And one day, when order breaks down into violence and chaos and starving hordes are roaming the land, you will be the one who can hold up your cleaver and say 'I did A Level Food Technology. I can save humanity!' So today, adults of tomorrow, we shall begin our study of the beast by investigating its life force. We are going to make blood pudding

Fillet *arranges the ingredients.*

Onions finely chopped, a kilo of diced pork fat, two metres of intestine, a litre of double cream, oatmeal, barley, salt, mace

Fillet *lifts a bowl filled with pig's blood on to the table.*

And here is our pig's blood. Now, this is an interesting fact. Pig's blood is identical to human blood by ninety eight percent. Isn't that a strange fact? We are only two percent different from a pig. Mint is dead. Mint, my comrade, your teacher, has fallen. We shall have a minute's silence at the end of the lesson but for now, contemplate this: GOD, WHY DID YOU MAKE US ONLY TWO PERCENT DIFFERENT FROM A PIG? Forgive me. I'm wreckage this morning. I loved Mint. Mint was an innocent. You get gallons of blood from each mature beast but here, I have just two litres

The great thing about this speech is that it is larger than real life. You can really enjoy thinking about how to play it and how to make the character tragically comedic and strangely weird. The style begins as that of a teacher standing in front of a class lecturing but then becomes strange and other-worldly.

The Wardrobe

Sam Holcroft

*This play presents a magical landscape in the back of an old Tudor
wardrobe in which British children from the last five centuries seek safety
from various dangers. The play contains about a dozen seemingly
unrelated scenes; we meet each character only once. As each scene
unfolds, we realize that it is a personal incident that is related to a
significant public event in British history. The location of the wardrobe
is moved in each scene. In this scene, it is located in a bedroom in
Kenwood House, Hampstead, North London, and the date is 5 May 1780.*

Dido Elizabeth Belle, *thirteen-years-old, is the illegitimate daughter of
Sir John Lindsay, a British Navy captain, and an enslaved woman whom
Sir John encountered while his ship was in the Caribbean.* **Dido** *is
mixed-race. She resides in the house of her childless great-uncle, William
Murray, Lord Mansfield. A decade earlier, Lord Mansfield, a leading
judge, passed a famous judgment in court freeing a slave from
imprisonment by his master on the basis that slavery was unsupported by
law in England and Wales (although this did not end slave trafficking in
Britain altogether). The door to the wardrobe opens, and* **Dido** *quietly
enters. She pushes aside the dresses hanging on the rail and clears a
space for herself. The afternoon sun filters through the ornamental holes
piercing her with shards of light. She kneels on the floor and clasps her
hands in prayer. She hesitates, strains to listen, and when satisfied that
nobody can hear her begins to pray.*

Dido   Dear God, my heavenly father, thank you for today. Thank you
for the good weather we enjoyed and for the birds outside my window.
Thank you most especially for the fat pigeon that comes to rest in the old
oak. I have named him Charlie. Fat Charlie. Thank you for coffee –
powerful, rich coffee. I'm grateful for the strong flavour that cuts through
my sluggish morning mouth. I'm grateful for the two hours work I did
this morning. I'm grateful for the pages I edited, and the progress I
helped Uncle William to make with his accounts. I'm grateful that you
can't get lead poisoning from stabbing yourself with a pencil. Thank you
for that lovely moment just now when I mouthed to Uncle William, 'I
love you,' and he mouthed in return, 'I love you too, My Dear.' I am so
grateful to have the love of this family. What else . . .? Oh yes, I'm so

grateful that I am no longer scared of bees. And thank you for this beautiful wardrobe, which my Uncle gave to me so I might hang my beautiful clothes in here. Thank you for the smell of the wood, and the reassuring feel of the panels under my knees holding me up. Thank you for a place I can come to when I need to be alone. Thank you also for the fact I could talk to Elizabeth for an hour about her upcoming trip to the Derby race and I didn't feel hopelessly dissatisfied that I will not attend. I am learning that the secret to happiness is not how successful you are, or what people say about you, or how you look, or whether your parents were married, but whether or not you can be thankful for what you have. And so, right now, in this moment, I am grateful to my Uncle and his wife for all they have done for me and rescued me from. Today I am so grateful that I am not enslaved upon a ship, as my mother was. I am so grateful to my Uncle that he struck down slavery in court. And because of him I live without fear of torture and oppression. I don't know why I've been dealt such a fortunate hand, but to whomever is responsible for my lucky, lucky fate I am truly, truly thankful. Even though my illegitimacy and the colour of my skin mean that I am not eligible to eat with the family at the table, or join their guests for dinner, or attend the Derby with Elizabeth, I am so thankful that the women do invite me to join them for coffee when supper is done. I am so grateful they afford me that kindness; they show me such unwavering generosity.

Suddenly she pulls a dress violently off a hanger and throws it down; she smacks the wall of the wardrobe in distress. She cradles her injured hand. She catches her breath. She clasps her hands in prayer once again.

Forgive me, father, forgive my ungratefulness. Forgive my indulgence, my impatience, my selfishness. (*Short pause.*) I'm grateful to the concept of gratefulness for giving me a way to encourage happy thoughts and feelings. Thank you for giving me a way out of the dark and into the light.

Dido *kneels in silence for a moment. She kisses her hands and raises them to the heavens. She stands and smoothes her dress. She stares into space for a moment, all enthusiasm lost, before bracing herself and exiting the wardrobe.*

You should enjoy undertaking some research into the background and the socially-expected behaviour of your character, Dido. There is plenty of information about the slave trade and off-stage characters and events that will inform how you bring this character to life. You have sneaked into this large wardrobe so that you can openly pray, and you are being as polite as you can to God, but every so often your anger and resentment bubble to the surface, which creates a dramatic tension within you. Imagine the dynamics the confines of a wardrobe will create and achieve that intimacy with your audience. This is a historical piece, but be sure to play it fresh and youthful; after all, you're only thirteen years old, and although the language is seemingly more formal than that of most contemporary youth characters, you should play it with the same instincts and qualities as you would a speech with a contemporary setting.

We Lost Elijah

Ryan Craig

This play takes place in a suburban family garden. The narrative moves back and forth in time, and centres on the disappearance of one of the family who, it turns out, is hiding in the shed all the time. This speech is by his sort-of girlfriend Grace, and it is from halfway through the play, when she gives Elijah the idea of hiding in the garden shed.

Grace ok . . . so we had this gerbil when I was around five. George.

Little ginger thing he was and cute as a plum and when we first got him, Kara and me, we made such a big fuss about him; grooming him and replenishing the straw in his hut so he was all cosy and happy. Mum was all like 'that bloody rodent's not coming anywhere near this house' so we put him in this shed . . . we had . . . way, way down at the end of the garden. One time George got out of his cage, escaped. We had the whole street out looking for him; shouting his name, crawling under cars . . . Kara and me were distraught, on and on we went saying how special he was to us and how we felt so guilty . . . furious with ourselves for not securing his cage properly. It killed us the thought we'd never see him again. So when our Uncle Eddie found him in a hedge nibbling at some sick outside number twelve we hugged him close and vowed to take extra special care of him from this day forth. After a bit though we started resenting him. Trudging all the way down the end of that garden, every morning, rain or shine . . . then one morning after it was bitter cold in the night . . . I went down to the shed to give George his feed and he was rock solid. Dead eyed. Frozen to the bone.

The important thing in this speech is you must simply play what is on the surface; let the subtext take care of itself. You are recalling the events that happened to George, and not imagining what might happen in the future. It is a speech that is focused towards a listener, Elijah, who you know very well. Therefore, there should be a familiarity conveyed towards the person who is listening to you.

Where I Come From: Scenes from Abroad by Mike Williams

Richard Nelson

This play is about a group of American high school students who are on a trip to London in 1987. They are staying in a small hotel in Russell Square, and they stay up all night discussing an incident that has happened between one of their teachers and one of the girls on the trip. The discussion of the incident leads them to share other stories about their parents and families, and this is one of them.

Emily My Mother once took me swimming in the reservoir. She said she wanted a kind of 'mother–daughter' memory.

So we're swimming in this sort-of lake, we get out to the middle and a little floating – dock, you know, with a diving board on it, we're hanging onto it, and she says – the sun's in my eyes now, so I can hardly see her face – she has planned this. So she says – she hates – my father. The things he's done to her, she won't go into, because she knows I'll still have to see him, if I wish. If I'm stupid enough is the implication. If I can stomach it, which – she can't anymore. But she understands he's my – but he's fucking anything that walks. Her words. So how much time will he really have for me. So – She's leaving him. Actually he was leaving her, but I only learn this later. Leaving him. Now I'm in the middle of a lake. This is all a plan, so I can't just walk away and slam my door. I hated her for that. For doing that to me. For taking that away – of just slamming my goddamn door. I didn't care that she was crying. I just started swimming back. So we drove home and I said shit to her. That's why I think I stayed with my father for the first six months or so. Even though I hated that, I knew he didn't want me, he made that clear, but I wanted to punish my Mother for telling me like that.

Emily finds this recent moment in her life extremely traumatic. As you journey through the speech, the emotional recall – as you picture the lake, the sun, the temperature, the feeling of being trapped in the water – becomes increasingly more intense. The young people in the play find telling their private stories to be in some way therapeutic, so you should convey a sense of this towards the end of the speech; although the act of describing the incident is in itself traumatic, the effect of it enables you to find a new inner strength.

This speech is written in American dialect, so you could try it with an American accent. If you want to listen to some young people speaking online to help you learn the accent, this particular character comes from Chicago, but a general American would do, as long as you keep it consistent.

Zero For The Young Dudes!

Alistair McDowall

This play takes place in a summer camp where the young campers are plotting a revolution. In this scene a group of them are serving a punishment by shovelling earth from one side of the camp to the other. One of them stops work for a few minutes to tell the others about his dream.

Do you like Harry Potter?

Dumbledore's the coolest!

I once had a dream where I was a wizard, cept it wasn't like Harry Potter, I wasn't at Hogwarts or anything, I was just here in the camp cept I had magic powers, and I was using them to zap all the guards and the counsellers and then I used my wand to bust the fences, some of the fences I could melt with a special spell I had, oh and also I was flying? And then we all got freed and all of us were running out of the camp all cheering and everyone was shouting my name because I was the hero, but then when we got outside everyone's head just suddenly started melting! Everyone stopped running and there was this kind of *fizzing* sound and then everyone's head was all just bubbling and popping like rice crispies and their eyes were drooping down their heads and their mouths went from big smiles to big frowns and everyone was like, grabbing at their heads saying No! No! Don't melt my head! And they all thought it was *me*, because *I* was the one with the magic! They were all looking up at me with their runny eyes saying Don't! Stop! Stop melting our heads! Why would you free us just to melt our heads?! And I'm like I didn't, I didn't! I'm trying to tell them it's not me, it's not my fault, but their ears have all melted so they can't even *hear* me! So I try to do a spell that'll make their heads go back to normal except now it's like all my magic is *gone*, I can't do magic anymore for some reason, but it's too late anyway because now everyone's head is just a big pink puddle on their necks and they're all falling down dead. And then the last one who still has half a head comes up to me and he was trying to keep the shape of it like he was trying to hold melting ice cream into some kind of structure and he looks at me with his eyes that are like dripping yolks and his mouth was all waxy like a candle and he just looks straight at me and just says—

Why?

. . .

And then he falls down dead like the rest.

. . .

. . .

. . .

What do you think that means?

You need to make really canny choices about when to breathe in this speech. The intonation will surprise you – for example, some lines end with question marks and you may not be expecting them. The situation you're describing is heightened, unreal, a story that unfolds in a dreamscape. The subject matter becomes darker as you move through the speech but be careful not to play this darkness as the imagery you describe will be more startling if you simply 'say what you saw' in a matter of fact way, and let the language take its effect on the audience.

Agent and Publisher Information

If you would like to find out more information about the professional or amateur performing rights for these plays, please contact the following agents and publishers:

42

First floor
8 Flitcroft Street
London WC2H 8DL
United Kingdom
http://www.42mp.com/
Tel: +44 (0) 20 7292 0554

Those Legs by Noel Clarke

THE AGENCY (LONDON) LTD

24 Pottery Lane
Holland Park
London W11 4LZ
United Kingdom
http://theagency.co.uk/
Tel: +44 (0)20 7727 1346

Boat Memory by Laline Paull
Cloud Busting by Helen Blakeman
Dirty Dirty Princess by Georgia Fitch
The Edelweiss Pirates by Ayub Khan Din
Frank & Ferdinand by Samuel Adamson
Gargantua by Carl Grose
Horizon by Matt Hartley
A Letter To Lacey by Catherine Johnson
Mugged by Andrew Payne
The Shoemaker's Incredible Wife by Federico García Lorca, translated by
    Lucinda Coxon
Shut Up by Andrew Payne
Success by Nick Drake

AJ LITERARY ASSOCIATES

Higher Healey House
Higherhouse Lane
White Coppice
Chorley
Lancashire PR6 9BT
United Kingdom
Tel: +44 (0) 1257 273148

Mobile Phone Show by Jim Cartwright

ALAN BRODIE REPRESENTATION

Paddock Suite
The Courtyard
55 Charterhouse Street
London EC1M 6HA
United Kingdom
http://www.alanbrodie.com/
Tel: +44 (0)20 7253 6226

Baby Girl by Roy Williams
Multiplex by Christopher William Hill

CAA

405 Lexington Avenue, 19th Floor
New York, NY 10174
USA
http://www.caa.com/
Tel: +1 212 277 9000

Alice by Heart by Steven Sater and Duncan Sheik
Children of Killers by Katori Hall

CAPERCAILLIE BOOKS

1 Rutland Court
Edinburgh EH3 8EY
Scotland
United Kingdom
http://www.capercailliebooks.co.uk/
Tel: +44 (0)845 463 6759

Blooded by Isabel Wright

CASAROTTO RAMSAY AND ASSOCIATES

Waverley House
7–12 Noel Street
London W1F 8GQ
United Kingdom
http://www.casarotto.co.uk/
rights@casarotto.co.uk
Tel: +44 (0)20 7287 4450

Blackout by Davey Anderson
Can You Keep a Secret? by Winsome Pinnock
The Chrysalids by David Harrower, after John Wyndham
Citizenship by Mark Ravenhill
Dust by Sarah Daniels
The Grandfathers by Rory Mullarkey
The Guffin by Howard Brenton
Prince of Denmark by Michael Lesslie
The Spider Men by Ursula Rani Sarma
Taking Breath by Sarah Daniels
Totally Over You by Mark Ravenhill

CURTIS BROWN

Haymarket House
28–29 Haymarket
London SW1Y 4SP
United Kingdom
http://www.curtisbrown.co.uk/
Tel: +44 (0)20 7393 4400

The Accordion Shop by Cush Jumbo
Almost Grown by Richard Cameron

Bassett by James Graham
Chatroom by Enda Walsh
Follow, Follow by Katie Douglas
Heritage by Dafydd James
Hood by Katherine Chandler
Hospital Food by Eugene O'Hare
Little Foot by Craig Higginson
The Monstrum by Kellie Smith
A Shop Selling Speech by Sabrina Mahfouz
The Snow Dragons by Lizzie Nunnery

FABER AND FABER

Bloomsbury House
74–77 Great Russell Street
London WC1B 3DA
United Kingdom
http://www.faber.co.uk/
Tel: +44 (0)20 7927 3800

Eclipse by Simon Armitage
Friendly Fire by Peter Gill
Gizmo by Alan Ayckbourn

INDEPENDENT TALENT GROUP

40 Whitfield Street
London W1T 2RH
United Kingdom
http://www.independenttalent.com/
Tel: +44 (0)20 7636 65656

Stone Moon by Judith Johnson
Tomorrow I'll Be Happy by Jonathan Harvey

JUDY DAISH ASSOCIATES

2 St Charles Place
London W10 6EG
United Kingdom
http://www.judydaish.com/
Tel: +44 (0)20 8964 8811

The Bear Table by Julian Garner
He's Talking by Nicholas Wright
My Face by Nigel Williams
Zero For The Young Dudes! by Alistair McDowall

KNIGHT HALL AGENCY

Lower Ground Floor
7 Mallow Street
London EC1Y 8RQ
United Kingdom
http://www.knighthallagency.com/
Tel: +44 (0)20 3397 2901

Cuba by Liz Lochhead
In The Sweat by Naomi Wallace and Bruce McLeod
Moonfleece by Philip Ridley
Pronoun by Evan Placey

LISA RICHARDS AGENCY

108 Upper Leeson Street
Dublin 4
Ireland
http://www.lisarichards.ie/
Tel: +353 1 637 5000

Angels by Pauline McLynn

MACNAUGHTON LORD REPRESENTATION

44 South Molton Street
London W1K 5RT
United Kingdom
http://www.mlrep.com/
Tel: +44 (0)20 7499 1411

Where I Come From: Scenes from Abroad by Mike Williams

METHUEN DRAMA

Bloomsbury Publishing
50 Bedford Square
London WC1B 3DP
United Kingdom
http://www.bloomsbury.com/
Tel: +44 (0)20 7631 5600

Asleep Under the Dark Earth by Sian Evans
Dead End by Letizia Russo, translated by Aleks Sierz
The Minotaur by Jan Maloney
Nuts by Fausto Paravidino, translated by Zachary Kinney
Pass It On by Doug Lucie
Status Update by Tim Etchells

MICHELINE STEINBERG ASSOCIATES

Suite 315
ScreenWorks
22 Highbury Grove
London N5 2ER
United Kingdom
http://www.steinplays.com/
Tel: +44 (0)20 3214 8292

The Bedbug by Snoo Wilson
The Black Remote by Glyn Maxwell

NICK HERN BOOKS

The Glasshouse
49a Goldhawk Road
London W12 8QP
United Kingdom
https://www.nickhernbooks.co.uk/
Tel: +44 (0)20 8749 4953

Burying Your Brother in the Pavement by Jack Thorne
The Wardrobe by Sam Holcroft

OBERON BOOKS

521 Caledonian Road
London N7 9RH
United Kingdom
http://www.oberonbooks.com/
Tel: +44 (0)20 7607 3637

DNA by Dennis Kelly

PBJ

22 Rathbone Street
London W1T 1LG
United Kingdom
http://www.pbjmanagement.co.uk/
Tel: +44 (0)20 7287 1112

Soundclash by Lenny Henry

ROCHELLE STEVENS AND COMPANY

2 Terretts Place
Upper Street
London N1 1QZ
United Kingdom
http://www.rochellestevens.com/
Tel: +44 (0)20 7359 3900

Generation Next by Meera Syal

ROSICA COLIN

1 Clarenville Mews
London SW7 5AH
United Kingdom
Tel: +44 (0)20 7370 1080

Lunch in Venice by Nick Dear
Starstone by Christian Martin, translated by Penny Black

SHANAHAN MANAGEMENT PTY LTD

Level 3 Berman House
91 Campbell St
Surry Hills
NSW 2010
Australia
Tel: +61 (0)2 8202 1800

Seventeen by Michael Gow

SUSAN STEIGER

60 East 42nd Street
47th Floor
New York, NY 10165
USA
Tel: +1 212 880 0865

Travel Club and Boy Soldier by Wole Soyinka

UNITED AGENTS

26 Lexington Street
London W1F 0LE
United Kingdom
http://www.unitedagents.co.uk/
Tel: +44 (0)20 3214 0800

After Juliet by Sharman Macdonald
Broken Hallelujah by Sharman Macdonald
Burn by Deborah Gearing
Discontented Winter: House Remix by Bryony Lavery

I'm Spilling My Heart Out Here by Stacey Gregg
Illyria by Bryony Lavery
It Snows by Bryony Lavery, and Scott Graham & Steven Hoggett for
Frantic Assembly
The Miracle by Lin Coghlan
More Light by Bryony Lavery
The Queen Must Die by David Farr
Ruckus in The Garden by David Farr
Same by Deborah Bruce
The Things She Sees by Ben Power, after Charles Boyle
Too Fast by Douglas Maxwell
A Vampire Story by Moira Buffini
We Lost Elijah by Ryan Craig

THE WRITERS' COMPANY

33 Oval Road
London NW1 7EA
United Kingdom
http://writerscompany.co.uk/
Tel: +44 (0)20 7184 5747

The Heights by Lisa McGee

THE WYLIE AGENCY (UK) LTD

17 Bedford Square
London WC1B 3JA
Tel: + 44 (0) 20 7908 5900

Just by Ali Smith
Take Away by Jackie Kay